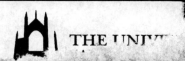

ScottishBallet

Forty years

ScottishBallet

Forty years

Mary Brennan

Saraband

Published by Saraband
Suite 202, 98 Woodlands Road
Glasgow G3 6HB, Scotland

www.saraband.net

ISBN-13: 978-1-887354-68-4

Printed and bound in the UK by Butler Tanner & Dennis Ltd.

1 2 3 4 5   12 11 10 09

Page 2: Sophie Martin and Erik Cavallari in George Balanchine's *Rubies* (© Merlin Hendy)

Contents

Breaking New Ground

MOVING HOUSE: COMING FULL CIRCLE

In 1969, a band of dancers led by the late Peter Darrell, packed their hopes – and their memories – into trunks and boxes and suitcases and moved house. All the way from Bristol, where they had proved their mettle as Western Theatre Ballet, over the border to Glasgow – and the promise of a new future for them, and for us, as the first incarnation of what is now Scottish Ballet.

In June 2009, a much larger group of dancers, led by Ashley Page, packed a new-found sense of artistic possibility into their hearts, minds and bodies as they too moved house. Out of the higgledy-piggledy West End warren of cramped studios that no longer fitted the growing needs and ambitions of a forward-looking national ballet company, and across the River Clyde to a new, purpose-built complex that appropriately connects Scottish Ballet with the legendary Tramway, a venue at the forefront of arts provision in the city. These dancers, along with administrative staff, the wardrobe department, technicians and music-makers, also took a precious store of memories with them – safeguarding connections with past milestones in an ongoing journey.

This book offers a selection of those memories, caught in the click of a camera shutter and held ever after – split-second fragments of a rich, eventful history that gains in national significance every day. For if Scottish Ballet's 40th anniversary is a celebration of the company and the talented individuals who have kept faith with it over the years, it's also a celebration of those members of the public who constantly proved – by coming to performances, buying souvenirs from the merchandising stall, or signing campaigning petitions – that dance, be it classical ballet or contemporary, has a place, indeed a home, in Scotland.

ABOVE: "DO IT THIS WAY, DARLING...!" PETER DARRELL, IN THE THICK OF REHEARSING THE COMPANY FOR HIS *TALES OF HOFFMANN* (1972, SEE PAGES 64–65).

When Peter Darrell accepted the invitation to relocate his Bristol entourage north, he nailed some very brave colours to the mast. His conviction that boldly imagined, well-made dance could thrive – find audiences and develop new ones – outside of the London enclave had been bolstered by the artistic (if not the financial) successes chalked up by Western Theatre Ballet. Giving Scotland its own, resident classical ballet company – capable of staging exciting new work in the cities but also ready to tour small-scale pieces to all points of the compass – swiftly became an unstinting commitment that would stay with him to the end of his life.

THESE PAGES: *GISELLE* (1971) WAS THE FIRST OF THE 19TH-CENTURY CLASSICS TO BE REVIVED BY 'THE DARRELL TOUCH'. HIS AIM WAS TO MAKE THE STORIES AND CHARACTERS RELEVANT TO MODERN AUDIENCES. ELAINE McDONALD (OPPOSITE), THE FIRST BALLERINA TO DANCE THE TITLE ROLE FOR SCOTTISH, PORTRAYED GISELLE AS AN ORDINARY, HAPPY GIRL WHO IS FATALLY BETRAYED IN LOVE. BELOW, HILARION IS CONFRONTED BY MYRTHA, QUEEN OF THE WILIS; ABOVE RIGHT, THE WILIS, VENGEFUL SOULS OF MAIDENS WHO DIED BEFORE THEIR WEDDING DAY.

That first Scottish decade was a distinctly heady one. Darrell had, during the twelve years of Western Theatre Ballet's existence, created a groundbreaking repertoire of dance-dramas that drew inspiration from post-war French cinema and the new British Theatre. He watched as the 'angry young men' who'd had enough of well-mannered plays set in blinkered drawing-rooms began giving voice to grittier realities – and reckoned it was time for ballet's classical technique to lend pointe (shoes) to uncompromisingly modern scenarios. He was alive to new trends in fashion and popular music, aware of the influence that television had on an increasing number of households. The resulting ballets were as up-to-the minute as any other art form or entertainment. If the 1960s were swingin' – ballet would swing, too.

Flick through some of the earliest photographs that are stored away in the archive, and you'll see a group of young dancers who radiate a bright, streetwise energy as well as a passion for dance. They've upped sticks to take part in a great adventure: they're going to be the first ever members of Scotland's national ballet company... Did it matter that they were, to begin with, shoehorned in beside the Scottish Opera in Elmbank Crescent? Whatever else might have been cramped, it wasn't style or ambition.

VARIETY – IN STYLE, CONTENT AND DESIGN – WAS A HALLMARK OF THE EARLY DAYS OF THE COMPANY. ABOVE: ART NOUVEAU SET DESIGN FOR *TALES OF HOFFMANN* (1972). OPPOSITE: NORIKO OHARA IN *THREE DANCES TO JAPANESE MUSIC* (1973). BELOW: *STREET GAMES* (1972).

Scottish Theatre Ballet

Arriving
Bellevue
Sunday...

by Ashley Killar
inspired by Per Paolo
Pasolini's film Theo

La Fête Étrange
based on the
Alain-Fournier novel
Le Grande Meaulnes
subject of
Albicocco's film
The Wanderer

ABOVE: POSTER FOR AN EXPRESSIONIST WORK BY ASHLEY KILLAR, WHO LATER JOINED THE ROYAL BALLET. OPPOSITE: A GRACEFUL DYING SWAN, FROM THE WORK OF THE SAME NAME, TAKEN FROM *SWAN LAKE*.

New work, lots of it, kept the repertoire topped up with fresh challenges for audiences and dancers alike. Some highlights from Western Theatre Ballet were carried over – Darrell's own *Ephemeron* was one. But the mood within this tight-knit group of cultural pioneers didn't really favour the safety net of recycling. Even when the call was for the company to tackle the established classics – those evergreen ballets that are the bread-and-butter mainstays of so many repertoires – Darrell wasn't inclined to follow the pack. His *Giselle* (1971) honoured the 19th-century choreography, but his interpretation was his own. And when his muse, the outstandingly gifted Elaine McDonald, danced the leading role she – like Darrell – saw *Giselle* in heart-rendingly everyday terms: an ordinary girl who loves, trusts and is betrayed by a wealthy man who conceals his commitment to another woman.

The Nutcracker, Swan Lake, Cinderella: in time these heritage works would also undergo the 'Darrell touch' – a process described by colleagues as 'scattering the stardust' – so that a meaningful humanity breathed fresh vitality into the traditions of a different era, and celebrated the power of dance to express deep emotions that range beyond words.

With *Tales of Hoffmann*, Darrell's flair for vivid storytelling produced one of the company's most popular works – indeed, this witty, original response to Offenbach's music was still being regularly revived, and still being acclaimed by audiences and critics alike, until the end of the 1990s. Jack Carter, who had been associated with the company in its Western Theatre Ballet days, provided another memorable hit with his *Three Dances to Japanese Music*, a gorgeously costumed, visually striking and athletically dynamic piece that was subsequently filmed and broadcast by Scottish Television.

ABOVE: ONE OF THE DRAMATIC BALLETS THAT WESTERN THEATRE BALLET BROUGHT TO SCOTLAND. *THE LESSON* (1963), CHOREOGRAPHED BY FLEMMING FLINDT, WAS INSPIRED BY A DARKLY MURDEROUS IONESCU PLAY. FLINDT, LIKE MANY OTHER CONTRIBUTORS TO THE REPERTOIRE, INTRODUCED A VALUABLE EUROPEAN PERSPECTIVE NOT FOUND IN OTHER UK COMPANIES OF THE TIME.

"I have danced many times with The Scottish Ballet and have always admired the dedication and enthusiasm of its dancers and management.

Scottish Ballet, as the company soon came to be called, was intent on making its own mark on the dance world, national and – hurrah! for the cheek of it – international. And so the company took to the road: toured the Highlands and Islands, the Borders and in between – then set off, with the help of a few famous friends, to take on the Antipodes. The long-haul Australasian tour of 1974 saw Margot Fonteyn and Ivan Nagy (then a premier danseur with American Ballet Theatre) become much, much more than just the kind of 'special guests' (and let's not pretend they don't exist!) who parachute in, wow audiences with a few well-chosen *fouttes* or *tours en l'air*, pick up the paycheque and retreat to the comforts of their hotel suite. Fonteyn, especially, seems to have fallen in love with Scottish Ballet during the course of the seven-week trip. She danced in every one of the 46 performances the company gave on a circuit that swept across Australia and on to New Zealand. Afterwards, she signed a poster image of herself with a hand-written message for Darrell: 'Dear Peter – It was you who made me do the tour, all my thanks. It has been wonderful. Love, Margot.' Her words marked the beginning of a truly warm and supportive relationship with Scottish Ballet.

LEFT: MARGOT FONTEYN'S ENTHUSIASTIC SUPPORT FOR SCOTTISH BALLET IS REFLECTED IN HER PROGRAMME NOTE. DARRELL'S *SCARLET PASTORALE*, BELOW, WAS CHOREOGRAPHED SPECIFICALLY FOR HER. OPPOSITE: MORE BEWITCHMENT – BOURNONVILLE'S *LA SYLPHIDE*, WITH NORIKO OHARA AS THE SYLPH AND NIGEL SPENCER AS JAMES.

Above: Joining up the dots — or rather, stringing together the decorative balls for the Kingdom of the Sweets, as designed by Philip Prowse for Act II of Darrell's *The Nutcracker*.

left: Graham Bart, a staggeringly sensual Bothwell in Darrell's *Mary Queen of Scots* (1976). Bart arrived in rehearsals having just stepped into Rudolf Nureyev's shoes by partnering Margot Fonteyn — at her behest — in a programme of pas de deux in Mauritius.

In 1975, Darrell showed his personal appreciation for the ongoing interest Fonteyn showed in a company that was so boldly – and successfully – punching above its weight. He choreographed *The Scarlet Pastorale* for her (see previous pages), a ballet that looked well beyond her 'received' persona of Romantic purity and allowed her to revel in divinely wicked decadence... with murder as her final, flamboyant move. Philip Prowse's designs, like the ballet itself, picked up on the renewed interest that was being shown in the drawings of Aubrey Beardsley. The effect was thrillingly dramatic.

More drama, off-stage as well as on, arrived when yet another legendary name appeared in a 1975 performance of *La Sylphide*: it was Rudolf Nureyev and he, like Fonteyn, clearly relished the energy that saw Scottish Ballet combine increasingly high standards of technique with an unstuffy, eager attitude to the hard work those standards entailed.

ABOVE: *PAS DE QUATRE*. A STEP INTO BALLET HISTORY – ANTON DOLIN RE-CREATED THIS RIVALRY BETWEEN CELEBRATED 19TH-CENTURY BALLERINA-DIVAS FOR A GALA AT THE KING'S THEATRE, GLASGOW, IN 1975.

Nureyev's fondness for dancing *La Sylphide* with Scottish Ballet encouraged the company to give him a gift (in 1976) of full Highland dress in Stuart tartan. His fondness for making his own costuming choices, however, saw him resplendent in a turquoise ensemble (illustrated on the programme cover overleaf) when he invited the company to be his 'backing group' during *Le Festival Noureev* in Paris the following year. Perhaps the several stars who came, either to dance or coach, were initially responding to Darrell's own standing. What brought them back, however, was the company's unswerving commitment to dance — and when that commitment meant small-scale touring across country... 'Have loyal audiences, will travel' became the watchword.

ABOVE: MERMAIDS ARE DANCING IN *THE WATER'S EDGE*, ROBERT NORTH'S CHOREOGRAPHY FOR SCOTTISH BALLET'S 10TH ANNIVERSARY PROGRAMME. OPPOSITE: DARRELL'S MUSE, ELAINE MCDONALD, IN A SIGNATURE WORK FOR BOTH, *FIVE RÜCKERT SONGS* (1978).

LEFT: PROGRAMMES BRING BACK MEMORIES, INCLUDING THE COMPANY'S SUPPORTING ROLE IN NUREYEV'S PARIS FESTIVAL, 1977.

BELOW: ACT II OF *NAPOLI* (1978), WITH PAUL RUSSELL AS GOLFO IN HIS UNDERWATER KINGDOM. SCOTTISH BALLET WAS THE FIRST UK COMPANY TO REVIVE THE FULL-LENGTH BOURNONVILLE BALLET IN 25 YEARS.

RIGHT: SALLY COLLARD-GENTLE TAKES
TIME BACKSTAGE TO COSSET HER FEET —
SHE'D ALREADY BEEN KEPT ON HER TOES
PARTNERING SPECIAL GUEST NUREYEV
IN PERFORMANCES OF *LA SYLPHIDE*
WITH SCOTTISH BALLET. BELOW: BULL'S
EYE! A CRACKED MIRROR DOESN'T DETER
A DANCER IN A HURRY.

OVERLEAF: SVETLANA BERIOSOVA
DELIVERS A MASTERCLASS IN POISE,
TECHNICAL FINESSE AND EXPRESSIVE
INTERPRETATION. SCOTTISH BALLET
BENEFITED FROM THE SUPPORT OF
PRESTIGIOUS GUEST TEACHERS LIKE
BERIOSOVA, WHO CHAMPIONED THE
COMPANY IN ITS EARLY DAYS.

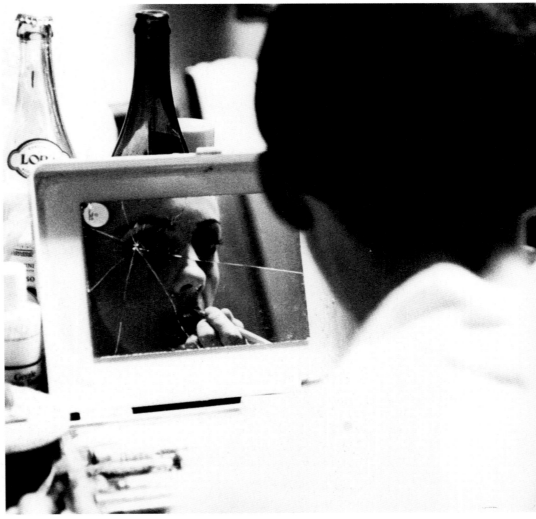

CAUSE FOR CELEBRATION: THE WARDROBE (BELOW) DOES THE FROTHY FROCKS FOR *SUCH SWEET THUNDER*, DARRELL'S CHOREOGRAPHY FOR THE 10TH ANNIVERSARY PROGRAMME.

The small-scale touring was replete with challenges, but rewarding in its own way; it might best be described as a labour of love. Imagine this: one week, you're not even on a purpose-built stage – it's more of a ledge. Lovingly polished by the rural hall-keeper and helpers, as a welcome. No one likes to complain that floor polish and pointe shoes are a potentially lethal combination. Just as no one has the heart to refuse the sandwiches, scones and cakes laid on before the performance... even though dancers prefer to perform on empty stomachs. Instead, the show goes on with as much élan as if the venue were Covent Garden and not a community centre where – and yes, this actually happened – the lights depended on somebody feeding a coin meter at the back.

News on the home front added to the feeling that the company had won hearts and minds across Scotland: premises had been found at 261 West Princes Street, Glasgow. The key to the door was handed over in 1978. The initial cost was £35,000, but necessary renovations added some £200,000 to the final fund-raising goal. This proved the truism that it's good to have Friends. And Scottish Ballet has, across the decades, been blessed with a loyal and resourceful band of Friends. Long before computers took the wrist-ache out of mail-shots, relays of Friends would turn up to stuff fliers into envelopes, their tongues ready to lick stamps, in between chats with passing dancers and members of staff, all of whom benefited from a nationwide network of impassioned support.

ABOVE: HRH THE QUEEN MOTHER SIGNS THE VISITORS' BOOK IN MARCH 1979 AT THE OFFICIAL OPENING OF 261 WEST PRINCES STREET (SEEN BELOW), THE COMPANY'S FIRST TRUE HOME.

OPPOSITE: NO CHOREO-
GRAPHIC BLOOMERS, BUT
A LOVELY STRETCH OF
IMAGINATIVE MISCHIEF
MADE JIRI KYLIAN'S
SYMPHONY IN D
A TEASING, PLEASING HIT
WITH AUDIENCES (1981).

The second decade for Scottish Ballet saw unsettled funding, bit by bit an encroaching constraint on budgets. The repertoire had fewer new works. Nonetheless, within 261 West Princes Street itself, the company's aspirations and ambitions remained as strong as ever. In-house talent was encouraged with a series of choreographic workshops, while the building itself underwent a further tranche of refurbishment to provide a rehearsal studio-cum-theatre.

The training initiatives that had always been an important element of the 'Ballet for Scotland' vision now took a new and exciting direction as plans to establish a Dance School of Scotland within Glasgow's Knightswood Secondary School came to fruition in 1983. The same year saw the company in Granada, with Elaine McDonald dancing what many considered her signature role in Peter Darrell's *Five Rückert Songs*. Darrell used the tour to do some window-shopping research for the full-length *Carmen* that premiered at the Edinburgh International Festival in 1985 (see pages 58–59).

BELOW: YOU *SHALL* GO TO THE BALL! DARRELL'S CINDERELLA SPREADS HER WINGS WHEN SHE MEETS HER PRINCE BEFORE HE LEADS HER INTO A PAS DE DEUX OF TRUE ROMANCE.

BELOW: A SMILING NORIKO OHARA STITCHES THE
RIBBONS ON HER POINTE SHOES FOR THAT EVENING'S
PERFORMANCE (SEEN AT RIGHT) OF DARRELL'S
GARDENS OF THE NIGHT .

BELOW: ...AND THE FEET ALSO HAVE IT IN THIS TRICKSY
LIFT FROM KYLIAN'S *SYMPHONY IN D*.

RELAXATIONS, ELEVATIONS.
CLOCKWISE FROM ABOVE:
PAOLO LOPES AND FIONA
BUSBY TAKE TIME OUT, PETER
DARRELL GIVES IMPROVING
NOTES, AND ROYALTY –
PRINCESS MARGARET (THEN
SCOTTISH BALLET'S PATRON)
AND PRINCESS DIANA –
OFFER POST-PERFORMANCE
CONGRATULATIONS.

OPPOSITE: DAME ALICIA
MARKOVA RAISES POINTS OF
TECHNIQUE IN A MASTER-
CLASS.

That *enfant terrible* of the 1980s' dance scene, Michael Clark, lodged his tongue firmly in his cheek when he choreographed the archly iconoclastic *Hail the Classical!* for a mixed bill that Darrell entitled *Gut Reactions*. The classical was, however, hailed – and revered – when Anton Dolin and John Gilpin memorably bestowed Mikhail Fokine's *Spectre de la Rose* on Scottish Ballet, for Vincent Hantam to dance. Hantam, clad in a faithful replica of Nijinsky's costume for the role, leapt into ballet history when he danced *Spectre*. Not many follow in Nijinsky's footsteps; fewer still do so with Hantam's exquisitely sensual grace.

Not a leap, but a leap year (and how to show something like that in a ballet?) – was what Darrell had in mind when he started preparations for a version of *Pirates of Penzance*. A few pre-publicity shots are all we have of *Pirates* (see overleaf). There simply wasn't the cash to do it, and it was shelved.

Spectre de la Rose. Opposite, Vincent Hantam, poised on the brink of legend in the role made famous by Nijinsky. Anton Dolin and John Gilpin coached Hantam in this bravura role that eludes many. His partner here and in the rehearsal shot below is Linda Packer.

THE PRISONERS

REBELS WITH CAUSE: *THE PRISONERS* (1983), OPPOSITE, WAS A 'BALLET NOIR' THAT SHOWCASED DARRELL'S FLAIR FOR UNCONVENTIONAL SUBJECTS AND CINEMATIC DANCE. MICHAEL CLARK, RIGHT, THE *ENFANT TERRIBLE* OF HIS TIME, CAME ON BOARD IN 1985 TO CHOREOGRAPH THE SUBVERSIVE *HAIL THE CLASSICAL!* DARRELL — IN CONTEMPLATIVE MOOD AT HOME, BELOW RIGHT — HAD PLANS TO DO A VERSION OF *PIRATES OF PENZANCE*. SADLY, THIS HAD TO BE SHELVED.

Darrell's death on December 2nd, 1987, created a maelstrom of emotions within the company. Scottish Ballet fans were shocked, of course. Yes, Darrell had renegotiated his role at the head of the artistic hierarchy, but at only 58 he surely had years of new work ahead of him...? The thought of no new Darrell ballets, ever, hit hard. But if the public mourned that loss, the grief that seized the company was a desperately complex, scarcely understood energy. Numbness at the passing of an anchoring, patriarchal presence coupled with a burning desire to do the best, no — better than that, the unattainable, perfect best, so that Darrell's lifelong vision wouldn't wither or tarnish. Anyone associated with Scottish Ballet in those aftermath days will know, but perhaps be reluctant to voice, the conflicting viewpoints and unsettling tensions that flooded the building as the company struggled to come to terms with the unexpected passing of its founder-choreographer.

Peter Kyle had already been named as chief executive. Any plans he might have made in preparation were overshadowed by the need to find a meaningful artistic focus for the company. Darrell's unstinting muse, Elaine McDonald, was the first of a succession of gifted artists – encompassing former dancers, choreographers, teachers and directors – who contributed their particular strengths to what was, in essence, a healing process for the company. Nanette Glushak breezed in, with a background in Balanchine that spurred the dancers to concentrate on technique. The Vinogradovs shuttled back and forth between Glasgow and the Kirov in Leningrad, forging a link that created a 'Perestroika Petrushka' full of biting satirical comment that reflected political changes in the USSR.

NEW STYLES, NEW CHALLENGES: ABOVE, REBECCA FLETCHER AND ROBERT HAMPTON EXPLORE THE LYRIC FLOW OF KYLIAN'S *FORGOTTEN LAND* (1990). ELSPETH SHAW (RIGHT) IS A KILTED DELIGHT IN GEORGE BALANCHINE'S LIVELY *SCOTCH SYMPHONY*. TOURING TO CHINA, BELOW. THE COUNTRY HAS BEEN REVISITED BY SCOTTISH BALLET IN THIS 40TH ANNIVERSARY YEAR.

ANNE CHRISTIE BRINGS
THE PERFUME OF THE
PAST ALIVE IN FREDERICK
ASHTON'S *FIVE BRAHMS
WALTZES IN THE STYLE OF
ISADORA DUNCAN*, A
REVOLUTIONARY FORCE IN
THE REALM OF MODERN
DANCE.

SPONSORSHIP IN CASH AND
KIND: VOLUNTEERS (BELOW)
HELP WITH JASPER CONRAN'S
DESIGNS (BELOW, RIGHT) FOR
THE SLEEPING BEAUTY; AND
JUDY MOHEKEY (BOTTOM) LET
THE TRAIN TAKE THE STRAIN
WHEN SHE WAS SPONSORED
BY SCOTRAIL.

And finally, Galina Samsova arrived, and rekindled fond associations for many of the long-serving stalwarts in the building. Scottish was a company she had danced with as a guest artist. When she and Andre Prokovsky had run their own company, they had commissioned Darrell to make work for them. That was, in fact, the provenance behind one of his most succint, dramatic works, *Othello*. At the end of her six-month stint as a visiting artistic director, Samsova was asked to stay on. Folk joked – but in a light-hearted, even hopeful way – about a 'Kirov-on-the-Clyde'. When confirmation came that yes, a new *The Sleeping Beauty* was planned, and yes, fashion designer Jasper Conran would be creating the sets, props and costumes, the company found itself making the news.

The Friends, meanwhile, had answered the wardrobe's call to help make the frocks... Bugle beads, it seemed, were the order of the day. Scatterings of the teensy-tiny, glinty shards needed to be sewn onto acres of rich devore velvets. The bugle bead defies

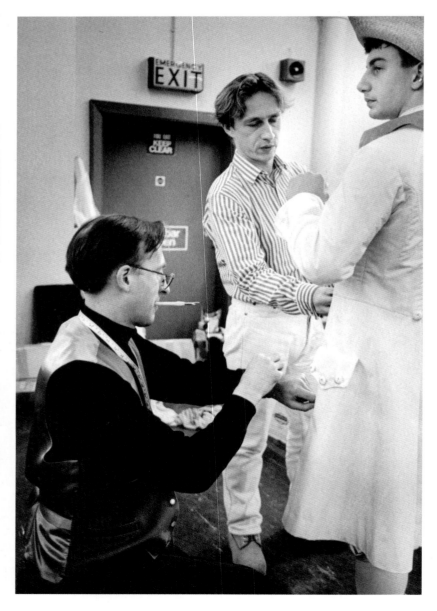

machining. It has to be attached by hand. Then – and indeed again, when he returned to design a subsequent *Swan Lake* – Conran marvelled at the nimble-fingered volunteer force who 'beaded for the Ballet'. A comparatively small budget blossomed into a sumptuous display of costumes. And Conran was heard to say 'you wouldn't get THIS at Covent Garden.'

Bit by bit, the jigsaw started to piece together again. But, just as Darrell had seen his vision blighted by a shift in political and economic dynamics, so too did the aspirational trio of Kyle, Samsova and Kenn Burke, a former (and much-loved) Scottish Ballet dancer who had gained leadership experience abroad and now put that expertise to good use as the assistant artistic director and driving force behind many of the small-scale initiatives.

Some memories never translate into photographs. And this particular book is not a definitive, blow-by-blow history of our national company. But throughout the 1990s there was a very real, and justifiable, fear that Scottish Ballet would be forced to close down. Funding shortfalls had already pushed budgets into deficit and – shades of what had nipped Darrell so badly – artistic ambitions were again being compromised by 'cash-efficient strategies' that threatened to undermine the identity, the autonomy, of the company. But, no matter what turmoils cast long shadows into the wings, the dance went on.

ABOVE: REHEARSING FOR *WINGS OF DESIRE*, LATER RENAMED *ESPRIT*, A BALLET SPONSORED BY BRITISH AEROSPACE AND TOURED BY SCOTTISH BALLET 2. THE PREMIERE WAS PERFORMED ON 27 MARCH, 1991, AT BRITISH AEROSPACE PRESTWICK IN THE PRESENCE OF THE QUEEN.

Sometimes that dance harked back to less troubled times: Darrell's ever-popular *Nutcracker*, his *Giselle, Chéri* and *Cinderella* all came centre-stage again. And again. But new works did enter the repertoire, among them the truly joyous Ashton piece *Five Dances in the Manner of Isadora Duncan*, made by him for Lynn Seymour who came, in person, to teach not just the steps but the very essence of this captivating solo. Robert North's mucho-macho *Troy Game* (see pages 76–77) saw the boys flex their pecs to fine effect. There was magic and mayhem – and tap-dancing Mechanicals – in Robert Cohan's inventive version of *A Midsummer Night's Dream,* while, for a brief time, Mark Baldwin (now heading up Rambert Dance Company) was installed as Choreographer-in-Residence. That Conran-designed *The Sleeping Beauty* was followed by a similarly opulent staging of *Swan Lake* that reverted to the original (and not the Darrell) scenario. Small-scale touring now hit the road as 'Scottish Ballet 2'. But, in 1997, the dancers were actually hitting the streets, asking the public to sign petitions in support of the company's survival. Samsova's resignation that year saw Kenn Burke shoulder acting responsibility for artistic direction, just in time to learn that funding for a full-length Christmas production of *Aladdin* (choreographed by Robert Cohan) was being withheld.

OPPOSITE: KENN BURKE
GETS HIS CLOGS ON (TOP
LEFT) AS WIDOW SIMONE
IN SIR FREDERICK ASHTON'S
LA FILLE MAL GARDÉE,
AND, MAIN IMAGE, WAYNE
SLEEP MAKES A GUEST
APPEARANCE AS THE
COMICAL BOOBY ALAIN.
'HULLAWRERR CHINAS',
BELOW LEFT: JACK MILROY
IN HIS FAMOUS 'FRANCIE'
GUISE BANTERS WITH THE
TAP-DANCING MECHANICALS
FROM ROBERT COHAN'S
*A MIDSUMMER NIGHT'S
DREAM*.

LEFT: GLAUCO DI LIETO
AND ARI TAKAHASHI IN
ROBERT NORTH'S *CARMEN*.

BELOW: "IT GOES LIKE
THIS..." ROBERT NORTH AT
THE PIANO WITH JON
ANDERSON, OF JETHRO
TULL FAME, DISCUSSING
MUSIC FOR *THE WATER'S
EDGE* (1979).

This desperate news travelled fast, and prompted a generous response from Birmingham Royal Ballet who said, 'Here, borrow one of our ballets', and handed over the whole kit and caboodle for Ashton's *La Fille Mal Gardée*. Scottish Ballet's own Friends decided that their Christmas present to the company would be Wayne Sleep, reprising his famous role as the comical numpty Alain — and if one of the technical crew proved to be allergic to horses, that didn't stop the wee Shetland pony appearing right on cue, stealing scenes...

Thirty years after the company had first arrived in Glasgow, its future frankly teetered on the brink of collapse. Not least because the age-old wrangle over classical ballet versus contemporary dance kept muscling in on the search for a new artistic director. Robert North, whose *Water's Edge* had been part of the 10th anniversary programme, took up the post in 1999, only to leave after three years. During that time Cohan's *Aladdin* did, finally, make it on stage. North re-staged his own *Light Fandango*, *Romeo and Juliet*, *Carmen* and the popular *The Snowman*. His departure rounded off what had been a decade and a half of administrative upheaval alongside valiant attempts to maintain standards and embrace change.

In September 2002, Ashley Page walked into 261 West Princes Street. You could say it was a 'Cinderella moment', for within a reassuringly short time, Page and Scottish Ballet proved to be the 'right fit'. More than that, it felt as though Page connected into Darrell's original vision for the company: dancers with strong technique both on and off-pointe; a radical approach to the classics; eye-catching, imaginative design. All adding up to a national ballet company that Scotland could enjoy at home and be proud of abroad.

Just as Peter Darrell had cast a musing eye over the important heritage ballets and then transformed them for modern audiences, without dumbing down either the choreography or the profound life issues in the narrative, so Page created first a new *The Nutcracker*, then a *Cinderella* and then *The Sleeping Beauty*, all of them strikingly innovative in ways that blew the cobwebs from weary traditions and refreshed the stories. Philip Prowse (then part of the remarkable creative triumvirate at Glasgow's Citizens Theatre) had frequently been Darrell's designer of choice. Page, too, had a trusted collaborative talent, Antony McDonald, sharing his mindset and translating bold ideas into wonderfully distinctive stage pictures.

NEW WAYS WITH OLD STORIES: ABOVE, SOPHIE MARTIN AND ERIK CAVALLARI IN REHEARSALS; OPPOSITE, 'WHOMSOEVER THIS SLIPPER FITS...' THE PRINCE (CRISTO VIVANCOS) BEGINS HIS SEACH FOR CINDERELLA IN ASHLEY PAGE'S VERSION OF THE CLASSIC. WATCHING ARE HIS ATTENDANTS (PAUL LIBURD AND GLAUCO DI LIETO) AND A HOPEFUL SISTER (DIANA LOOSMORE). RIGHT: BETHANY KINGSLEY-GARNER IN PAGE'S *THE SLEEPING BEAUTY*.

As Page's first decade with Scottish Ballet progresses, it already has the exhilarating, venturesome feel to it that made the company's initial, pioneering years so special and remarkable. Bravura works by Balanchine and Forsythe have come into the repertoire – taxing, technically demanding works that have powered up the mental and physical resources of the dancers, burnishing them into a world-class company capable, it seems, of anything. Stephen Petronio's raunch, all fast and feisty...? Bring it on! Krzysztof Pastor's lyrically expressive style...? Intelligent bodies will bend to his bidding.

Page's own choreography has the company run the whole gamut from edgy/sexy angularities and off-kilter pointe-work to softly tender (but far from easy) moves. Each new piece he makes on the dancers extends their understanding – of their innate abilities and of movement itself – just that bit further than the last. And whether he's at the director's desk, planning future seasons, or in the studio working through new steps, he can give free rein to artistic ambitions, knowing that he has a company ready to devour difficulty and make excellence the default setting.

MODERN MASTERY: OPPOSITE, EVE MUTSO RADIATES POISE AND PANACHE IN BALANCHINE'S *RUBIES*; ABOVE, LOUISA HASSELL KICKS OUT THE JAMS IN PETRONIO'S *RIDE THE BEAST*; AND BELOW: IREK MUKHAMEDOV RENEWED THE WORKING ASSOCIATION HE HAD WITH ASHLEY PAGE AT THE ROYAL BALLET WHEN HE MADE GUEST APPEARANCES AS DROSSELMEYER IN PAGE'S *THE NUTCRACKER*. CLAIRE ROBERTSON IS MARIE, THE YOUNG HEROINE.

ABOVE: JUNIOR ASSOCIATES: A GIGGLE OF FUTURE SWANS? OPPOSITE, BELOW: THE BACK-LOT STORAGE AT 261 WEST PRINCES STREET, A VAST ALADDIN'S CAVE OF PROPS, SETS AND TECHNICAL EQUIPMENT CAPABLE OF TRANSFORMING ANY STAGE INTO A SCENE OF DREAMS. OPPOSITE ABOVE AND BELOW RIGHT: ORDERLY STACKS OF POINTE SHOES AND ROWS OF TUTUS AND COSTUMES, CAREFULLY MAINTAINED BY THE WARDROBE STAFF.

Meanwhile, there aren't enough hours in the day for the outreach team and education unit to meet all the requests for workshops and lecture–demonstrations. Alongside training initiatives that have encouraged talented young dancers – some of whom have graduated to professional careers with Scottish Ballet – the company has developed a whole roster of activities with ordinary members of the public in mind.

You may not need to know a thing about dance to enjoy it or to appreciate a performer's grace, athleticism, or expressive physicality that can speak, with wordless eloquence, of our shared humanity. But being let in on the behind-the-scenes life of a ballet company – watching a rehearsal, going on a guided tour of the backstage domain of scenery, props and wardrobe, or just listening to dancers talking about what they do – can make a subsequent visit to the ballet all the more rewarding.

Would knowing some of the trade secrets spoil the illusion? On the contrary, being in on the 'tricks' really brings all of us closer to the flesh-and-blood resourcefulness and hard work that underpin everything our national ballet company does. And whether it's a workshop for children, a pre-performance talk about the music, or the development of online resources for schools, the aim is always the same: to make Scottish Ballet open, accessible and meaningful to all ages, and in as many parts of the country as possible.

ABOVE: ASHLEY PAGE IN
REHEARSAL.

OPPOSITE: SCOTTISH
BALLET'S POSTER FOR THE
40TH ANNIVERSARY TOUR
FEATURES SOPHIE MARTIN
AND ERIK CAVALLARI IN
THE WITTILY APPROPRIATE
RUBIES, BY BALANCHINE.

RIGHT: EVEN THE
FURNITURE CATCHES FIRE
IN *CHEATING*, *LYING*,
STEALING, ASHLEY PAGE'S
HIGHLY CHARGED
RESPONSE TO A TALE OF
SEX, LUST AND BETRAYAL
BY HANIF KUREISHI.

It's forty years since historic steps were taken to give Scotland its own ballet company. Four decades of triumphs and crises, and of remarkably loyal commitment, not just from dancers and staff, but from audiences and sponsors too. And never far from the heart of Scottish Ballet has been a degree of stubborn pride that refused to let the artistic hopes and creative promise of that 'Gang of '69' just fade away, be compromised, or die.

When Darrell and his dancers arrived in Glasgow, 'home' was in someone else's house; the group initially camped out at Scottish Opera's headquarters. It took almost a decade before the company had the key to their own front door, and for many, 261 West Princes Street will always hold sway over their memories, whether fond or poignant. But despite everyone's best efforts at upgrading and redesigning every nook of available space, the building was never going to morph into a Tardis. Long before this 40th anniversary loomed, there was too little space in the building for the business of dance-making, let alone to house mementoes of the past.

Box after box of archive material found a safe home on the Special Collection stacks at the University of Glasgow's library. Now many more boxes crammed with photographs, programmes and valuable documentation have been packed and moved. But this time their destination was Scottish Ballet's new, purpose-built complex at Tramway. In years to come, someone will doubtless do as we have done: sift through countless images, catching sight of a past that is witness to the timelessness of this cherished art form. And they'll see, as we hope you will in the pages of this book, that Scottish Ballet is forever home to all that is best and bravest in dance.

Memorable Images

1969–2009

PREVIOUS PAGE:
JARKKO LEHMUS AND CLAIRE ROBERTSON IN REHEARSAL

It's the moment when the theatre is empty, hushed and still. The afternoon's rehearsals are over. The dancers are resting in their dressing rooms, before putting on make-up and costumes for that evening's performance of William Forsythe's *Artifact Suite* (see pages 156–65).

Let's try that move again... Jarkko Lehmus and Claire Robertson take time to run through some of the steps for a very special audience of one: the photographer who freezes their artistry in the blink of a lens, and so saves it for posterity. There is a fabulous magic, as well as an archive of memories, in photographic images of dance. The camera bears witness to prowess – the buoyantly high jumps, the crystalline poise of a balance, the sheer muscular strength of a smoothly rising lift – that we, the audience, can sense as it happens but never actually see in minute, split-second detail.

Today's dancers are akin to Olympic athletes in their training and technique. But they are also required to show graceful purity of line in abstract works, or imbue narrative ballets with expressive characterisation and emotional depth. They do this for our delight, honing skills and interpretation, usually behind closed doors; sometimes unseen, except by themselves when they check out their own reflections in the studio mirror. And when they confide their efforts, their ongoing journey towards a personal best, to the watchful camera, which then, in turn, releases the image to us... our pleasure in the dance is magnified, enhanced.

Perhaps, as you turn the pages of this book, tracing how Scottish Ballet has kept faith with the artform of dance across four decades, you might send silent thanks to the many talented and sensitively attuned photographers who have filled the empty frames with lasting memories.

OPPOSITE: *SUCH SWEET THUNDER*

The title of this ballet comes from a jazz suite, composed by Duke Ellington and Billy Strayhorn in 1957, that created musical vignettes of various Shakespearean characters. Peter Darrell homed in on this for his contribution to Scottish Ballet's 10th Anniversary programme, a triple bill entitled *Underground Rumours*. But then, typically, he edged the jazzy joke just a little bit further, and gave a slyly witty Hollywood twist to the Shakespearean roles.

Among the double identities that Darrell concocted for *Such Sweet Thunder* (1979) were Othello/Sydney Poitier (danced by Paul Russell), Oberon/Liberace (Paul Tyers), Titania/Marilyn Monroe (Sally Collard-Gentle) and Hamlet/Elvis Presley (Peter Mallek). Lady Macbeth he envisaged as Rita Hayworth in her screen success, Gilda. And so Elaine McDonald (opposite) sashayed into view, all striking auburn hair, slinky black frock and long, long gloves that concealed a clever reference to that indelible spot of blood that finally drove Lady M mad. Ellington himself said of Lady Macbeth: 'We suspect she had a little ragtime in her soul.' Darrell agreed, and McDonald stripped off the gloves to give it free rein on stage.

OPPOSITE: PETER DARRELL'S *CARMEN*

Peter Darrell's three-act version of *Carmen*, with Christine Camillo in the title role, had its premiere at the Edinburgh International Festival in 1985. The piece was subsequently scaled down to a one-act ballet that was performed on 21st October, 1987, to mark the official opening of the Studio Theatre at Scottish Ballet's headquarters at 261 West Princes Street. This was the last work that Darrell made for the company before his death just six weeks later.

Scottish Ballet has performed three very different versions of *Carmen* over the years. In 2001, the then artistic diector Robert North staged a full-length choreography with a new score from Christopher Benstead with guitars, a piano accordion and an anvil in the orchestral ranks, alongside two singers who brought echoes of flamenco to the mix. For the third *Carmen*, Richard Alston's (2009), see pages 174–79.

OPPOSITE: AUGUST BOURNONVILLE'S *LA SYLPHIDE*

Bournonville's ballet of 1836 is one of the landmarks in classical ballet history, not just a truly Romantic narrative – a young Scots lad is lured away on his wedding day by an ethereal sylph, whom he is then tricked into destroying – but part of the revolution that brought pointe-work centre-stage, not as a gimmick but an essential part of ballet technique.

Scottish Ballet's love affair with the wonderfully beguiling sylph saw the ballet become a popular favourite in the repertoire, and a much-appreciated vehicle for star attractions like Margot Fonteyn and Rudolf Nureyev, who were guest artists with the company on several occasions. And if Nureyev insisted on bringing his own highly individual costume (vibrant turquoise velvet jacket and vividly matching tartan kilt, see page 24), his committed support of Scottish Ballet excused any eccentricities in his notion of Highland dress... The company's own ballerinas also made their mark in this ballet: Elaine McDonald, Noriko Ohara, Sally Collard-Gentle and Anne Christie (opposite) all danced the sylph to great effect, while Madge, the malevolent witch, was often portrayed in fine cackling fettle by Gordon Aitken, in madly ratty wig and full, hag-like make-up. Hans Brenaa, a ballet master and Bournonville specialist from the Theatre Royal in Copenhagen, came to Glasgow in 1973 to ensure that Scottish Ballet's revival of *La Sylphide* was true to the choreographic detail and spirit of the original.

OPPOSITE: PETER DARRELL'S *CHÉRI*

First performed in 1980 at the Edinburgh International Festival, Peter Darrell's *Chéri* (see also page 84) was based on the passionate, tragic novel by Colette in which Léa, a courtesan, falls for a spoiled, manipulative younger man, Chéri. Their steamy, stormy affair epitomises bohemian 1920s Paris. Darrell's ballet was set to a specially commissioned score by David Earl, with design by Philip Prowse. This image shows Chéri with his fiancée, the young socialite Edmée, danced by Paul Tyers and Eleanor Moore, who are married in real life. Paul Tyers danced many leading roles with Scottish Ballet before being appointed Ballet Master and, in 2005, Deputy Artistic Director. In association with the Royal Scottish Academy of Music and Drama, he has been instrumental in setting up the new degree course in Modern Ballet, of which he is Artistic Director.

OVERLEAF: *TALES OF HOFFMANN*

Elaine McDonald (page 64) reigns supreme as Giulietta, the elegantly seductive courtesan who almost steals Hoffmann's soul, as well as his heart, in Act III of Peter Darrell's richly inventive story ballet (1972) about a hapless poet, his disastrous love affairs, and the 'evil genius' that stalks him like a malevolent shadow.

Noriko Ohara (page 65) in captivating form as Olympia, the lifelike mechanical doll. Hoffmann, duped by special glasses into thinking she's alive, is totally smitten. His folly is enough to make the doll's creator Spalanzani (Gordon Aitken) and his helpers positively jump for joy. Music by Offenbach, arranged and orchestrated by John Lanchberry, and ravishing designs by Alistair Livingstone complemented Darrell's ideas perfectly: *Tales of Hoffmann* proved a hit not just for Scottish Ballet, but for the international companies who took it into their own repertoires.

Opposite and overleaf: Peter Darrell's *The Scarlet Pastorale*

By 1975, when Peter Darrell created this ballet for her, Margot Fonteyn had already shown a remarkable degree of support for what was a relatively new company – and one that had, moreover, dared to build its reputation and repertoire beyond the London dance-scene coterie and the Covent Garden stage, where she was ever a star attraction. As well as performing as a guest artist, Dame Margot (as she then was) thrilled fans by arriving to help celebrate the launch in October 1975 of the Edinburgh Branch of the Friends of Scottish Ballet. A fortnight later, at the King's Theatre in Edinburgh, Fonteyn, partnered by Augustus van Heerden (opposite, left), danced in the premiere of *The Scarlet Pastorale*.

The idea behind the piece had come from the Aubrey Beardsley illustrations that Darrell had seen in an edition of the Yellow Book. The drawings spoke of sensuality, decadence and a kind of evil that would coolly – even cruelly – kill the thing it loved if that was the only way to keep revelling in the pleasures of life. For once, vice would be seen to triumph over virtue. And Fonteyn's initial image of purity would be seen as merely masking a thoroughly wicked, and, as it happened, murderous disposition... A twist in the tale that Fonteyn enjoyed to the full, dancing this 'dark self' with a wonderfully exotic energy that positively oozed the inky-black seduction that Beardsley had outlined on paper. The designs, by Philip Prowse, captured the 'Beardsley look' with a witty flourish, which is evident in the fantastically costumed party scene (shown overleaf).

MEMORABLE IMAGES

Opposite: Peter Darrell's *Swan Lake*

Long before iconoclastic choreographer Matthew Bourne ruffled feathers with his all-male swans in his contemporary interpretation of 1995, and indeed well before the idea of refreshing the 'heritage classics' with the kind of storytelling that would engage modern audiences in the latter half of the 20th century, Darrell presented a *Swan Lake* (1977) that outraged some, but enthralled and delighted thousands more.

His concern, as always, was to show that classical ballet wasn't some archaic form best kept shrouded in cobwebs of nostalgia. And so his Prince Siegfried encountered his Swan Princess, the pure and lovely Odette, in an opium-induced dream. Shock, horror! An archetypal 'chevalier noble' as a druggie... Prince or no, this Siegfried was – despite the period costume, the courtly protocols and set-piece divertissements – caught up in a situation that those watching could recognise. Lonely, bored, at odds with the world around him, Siegfried was vulnerable to whatever Benno, his best friend – a 'Dark Angel' substitute for the customary evil magician, Rothbart – suggested. Benno, however, not only provides the opium, he provides the girl, Odile, who in Act I so beguiles the susceptible Siegfried that, in his mind-altered state, he transforms her into the ideal of Odette. By moving the famous 'Black Swan' pas de deux from Act III to Act I, Darrell enabled Tchaikovsky's music to revert to its original 1877 sequence: probably the most genuine tribute paid to *Swan Lake* in what was its centenary year.

The production stayed in the Scottish Ballet repertoire for several years and proved a showcase for many of the company's leading ballerinas who took on the double role of Odette/Odile. Among them was Noriko Ohara (opposite). A new production, with designs by Jasper Conran and a more conventional scenario, was staged in 1995 by the then artistic director, Galina Samsova.

Among the strongest, fondest memories people take away from ballets are the musical ones. Just a few bars, heard by chance in another context, can recollect all the happy sensations of watching a dance, of being caught up in the unfolding story – as in *Beauty and the Beast* (pages 72–73) – or of feeling the pulse race to the dynamic, percussive thrust that is Robert North's *Troy Game* (overleaf).

When Peter Darrell made his 1969 ballet *Beauty and the Beast*, he asked Thea Musgrave to compose a new, dramatically atmospheric score that would not only involve orchestral playing but incorporate a tape of pre-recorded sound. Few choreographers were, at the time, thinking in terms of electronic soundscapes. But Darrell, who had also used The Beatles' music for *Mods and Rockers* (1963) and made the first ever ballet for television, *Houseparty* (for the BBC in 1964), always saw Scottish Ballet as a company willing to push artistic boundaries, to be bold, to take risks. A version of *Beauty and the Beast*, by John Cranko (to music by Ravel), came briefly into the company's touring repertoire in 1973. Neither ballet has been revived in recent years.

From the first moment, in August 1991, that Glasgow audiences heard the insistent Batacuda rhythms of Bob Downes's score for *Troy Game* – and then saw a clutch of Scottish Ballet's male dancers storm on, flexing their pecs and ready for all-out athletic action, it was clear that North's choreography had scored a palpable hit. Aberdeen, Inverness and Edinburgh were soon similarly wowed by a display of swaggering, sometimes mischievous macho gamesmanship that was, in this revival, every bit as fresh and playful as when it was premiered by London Contemporary Dance Theatre in 1974. The images (overleaf) show a fine body of men taking North's precisely synchronised moves in their stride.

OPPOSITE: PETER DARRELL'S *OTHELLO*
A moment's pause in the wings, a look of intense concentration, as Lizst's *Faust* Symphony beckons Michael Crookes onstage in *Othello*, Darrell's dance-drama version of the Shakespearean tragedy.

OPPOSITE: ANDRÉ PROKOVSKY'S *ANNA KARENINA*; BELOW: PETER DARRELL'S *SWAN LAKE*

Noriko Ohara (opposite) in the opulent furs of Anna Karenina. André Prokovsky's full-length ballet of the same name, set to music by Tchaikovsky, was given its UK premiere by Scottish Ballet in 1993. Kirov stars Olga Likhovskaya and Andrei Jakolov took the leading roles of the ill-fated lovers at some performances, but it was Scottish Ballet's own Ohara who was the Anna on the poster, the programme cover and publicity material.

Another Kirov connection (below): Galina Mezentseva took leave of absence from her home company, the Kirov, to join Scottish Ballet as a guest artist. Here she's in the swan costume of Odette/Odile in *Swan Lake*, having previously made her debut with Scottish Ballet as the Sugar Plum Fairy in Darrell's *The Nutcracker* on 29th December, 1990.

OPPOSITE: *LA SYLPHIDE*
The ethereal sprites in *La Sylphide* epitomised a certain elusive magic in the Romantic imagination,
and were habitually garbed in the white of the '*ballets blancs*'.

BELOW: GALINA SAMSOVA'S *THE SLEEPING BEAUTY*
The fairies below, by contrast with the sylphs, are Technicolor beauties in tutus of gorgeous devoré velvet
with ornately hand-crafted beadwork. These costumes were designed by coutourier Jasper Conran for the
1994 production of *The Sleeping Beauty*, staged for Scottish Ballet by the artistic director Galina Samsova.

OPPOSITE AND BELOW: PETER DARRELL'S *CINDERELLA*

John Fraser's designs for Peter Darrell's *Cinderella* underlined the fairy tale's connection with magical woods, nature and hidden beauty by creating sets and costumes that reflected the visual opulence of the Art Nouveau period while playing with the idea of people hiding their true selves behind masks. The Prince (seated) watches as Dandini organises the preparations for the masked birthday ball – the little cooks have already danced on with splendid cakes – while (opposite) Dandini, having swapped disguises with the Prince, spreads one of the gossamer wings he will wear to the ball, where everyone else will also resemble gorgeous moths, butterflies and insects. And where everyone will mistake him for the Prince – all except Cinderella, of course.

OVERLEAF: TO HAVE AND TO HOLD
On page 84, Paul Tyers and Elaine McDonald in Darrell's *Chéri*. Jesus Pastor and Tomomi Sato (page 85) cut loose in an iconic image that was featured on a tour poster.

OPPOSITE AND FOLLOWING PAGES: REHEARSAL

Behind closed doors, wearing a variety of leotards, sweatshirts, jogging pants, legwarmers – layers that will be peeled away as bodies begin to sweat with effort – the dancers in Scottish Ballet rehearse and rehearse to make the most challenging moves look effortless on stage. This is the bridging point. The intense process through which a choreographer's ideas become flesh and blood, where bodies are pushed to achieve just that little bit more height in a jump... speed on a turn... drama in a lift.

These are the moments the public rarely sees. Moments when the engagement with new challenges are, actually, a private matter for dancers and choreographers alike. So for the company to grant a photographer access to these sessions is generous. And then to allow us to glimpse behind-the-scenes images, even those that might reveal what the rigour of rehearsal exacts from minds as well as bodies, is even more so.

In fact, there is an unparalleled beauty in these rehearsal shots. Something about the lack of influencing costume, the very dressed-down nature of studio clothes that seems to celebrate the dancer's art in a very immediate and affecting way.

Opposite: Paul Liburd lifting Tama Barry.

ABOVE AND OPPOSITE: TAKING FLIGHT
Adam Blyde in rehearsal.

OVERLEAF: POINTE-ING THE WAY
Amy Hadley, Nathalie Dupouy, Luisa Rocco and Quenby Hersh.

OPPOSITE AND ABOVE: PERFECT GRACE
Tama Barry and Sophie Martin.

OPPOSITE AND ABOVE: FLUID MOVES
Tomomi Sato and Adam Blyde.

ABOVE AND OPPOSITE: REHEARSAL SEQUENCES
Above, Will Smith and Martina Forioso, with Sophie Martin and Tama Barry in the background.
Opposite, Daniel Davidson and Martina Forioso.

ABOVE: FLYING HIGH
Diana Loosmore.

BELOW AND OVERLEAF: GESTURE AND NUANCE
Claire Robertson and Adam Blyde (below), and overleaf, Claire Robertson and Cristo Vivancos.

The company in George Balanchine's *The Four Temperaments*, which was first staged in 1946
by New York City Ballet and entered Scottish Ballet's repertoire in 2004.

Balanchine's *Episodes* is a superb work that is rarely performed, partly because of its difficult choreography, but also because the music, by Webern, is just as challenging in its complexities. Scottish Ballet became the first UK company ever to dance this piece, bringing it centre stage at the Edinburgh International Festival in 2005. Below, Paul Liburd and Patricia Hines lead in the third part of *Episodes*. Opposite, Eve Mutso and Erik Cavallari in Balanchine's *Agon*, set to music by Stravinsky and described at the time (1957) as 'an existential metaphor for tension and anxiety'.

BELOW AND OPPOSITE: DIVINE BALANCHINE

If the opening notes of Stravinsky's music send a frisson of anticipation through dance audiences, Balanchine's choreography for *Apollo* does not disappoint. Below, at the Edinburgh International Festival 2005, Erik Cavallari (right) was the young god; his three Muses were Eve Mutso, Claire Robertson and Soon Ja Lee. Opposite, Sophie Martin, Luciana Ravizzi and Martina Forioso are the Muses to Cristo Vivancos' *Apollo*.

Eve Mutso proves the epitome of a
Balanchine ballerina as she holds a
breathtaking balance in *Rubies*.

OPPOSITE AND BELOW: JEROME ROBBINS'S *AFTERNOON OF A FAUN*
Luisa Rocco and Christopher Harrison as the young dancers in Robbins's *Afternoon of a Faun*, a reflection on Nijinsky's famous ballet that turns it into a reverie on the art of dance itself.

ASHLEY PAGE'S *THE NUTCRACKER*

Page's *The Nutcracker* plunged into the darker reaches of Hoffmann's original story to give us a stylish baddie in the scheming Mouserink (seen opposite, Diana Loosmore, with the Nutcracker Doll in her clutches). Her best laid plans go properly awry however – the Nutcracker Doll is brought to life (below; Glauco di Lieto).

PREVIOUS PAGES, THESE PAGES AND OVERLEAF: ASHLEY PAGE'S *CINDERELLA*

In 2005 Ashley Page and designer Antony McDonald created a new version of *Cinderella* that was as much a moral tale as it was a true romance. On the previous pages, exotic princesses do some last minute primping for the ball (left to right: Limor Ziv, Nathalie Dupouy, Kara McLaughlin, Victoria Willard). Opposite, bad treatment from Cinderella's stepmother (Eve Mutso) and stepsisters (Diana Loosmore and Patricia Hines). Below, Cinderella (Claire Robertson) turns, hopefully, to her father (Jarkko Lehmus) for support against her new 'family', whose cruelty is matched by their appallingly awful taste. Overleaf, Martina Forioso (page 120) as one of the four seasons who are at the beck and call of Cinderella's godmother (Soon Ja Lee, page 121).

PREVIOUS PAGES AND LEFT: ASHLEY PAGE'S *THE SLEEPING BEAUTY*
Aurora's christening is shown in a scene from Act I of *The Sleeping Beauty* on pages 122–23. The fairies have just given the baby their gifts, and the mood is one of golden celebration.

Left: Hell hath no fury like a wicked fairy who's been left off the list of special guests. Carabosse (Limor Ziv) vows deadly vengeance on the newborn child, as Aurora's father (Jarkko Lehmus) and mother (Eve Mutso) look on in horror.

KRZYSZTOF PASTOR'S *ROMEO AND JULIET*

When Krzysztof Pastor choreographed a new version of *Romeo and Juliet* (2008), he updated each episode in the narrative to a crucial period in 20th-century history, reinforcing the message that bigotry, gang warfare and political conflicts are what doom the star-crossed lovers in Shakespeare's play – and in our modern times.

On the previous pages (126–27), the Capulets – black-shirted supporters of Mussolini in 1930s Italy – are seen in hot-headed confrontation with the more liberal-minded Capulets. Opposite: Love at first sight. Erik Cavallari (Romeo) and Sophie Martin (Juliet) in a rapturous pas de deux... behind the backs of her family, who would not approve.

PREVIOUS PAGES: TRAGEDY UNFOLDS IN *ROMEO AND JULIET*
The scene is post-war Italy (previous pages, 130–31), the future should be bright,
but Mercutio and Tybalt lie dead and all the old enmity between the Capulets and
Montagues is surfacing again.

ABOVE AND OPPOSITE: AND IN THEIR DEATH THEY WERE NOT DIVIDED
Tomomi Sato and Tama Barry (above) as Juliet and Romeo in the final moments of Pastor's ballet.
Opposite: Sophie Martin and Erik Cavallari in the same roles.

OPPOSITE: REFLECTION
Eve Mutso manages to be wonderfully elegant even when cornered.

OPPOSITE: STEPHEN PETRONIO'S *RIDE THE BEAST*

Stephen Petronio's *Ride the Beast* takes its title from a speedboat ride that hurtles across New York Harbour in a trip that promises high speeds, pumping music and great views. This could actually be a description of Petronio's choreography, with its fast, energetic action set to music by Radiohead and with fabulous costumes, designed by Benjamin Cho, that cling or reveal in a wittily provocative fashion.

There's no cut-and-dried narrative to the piece. Instead, Petronio uses the Radiohead songs, which are favourite tracks for him, as a backdrop for little episodes that reflect aspects of life in a city. Adam Blyde (opposite) is, at one point, a rather slithery, sinister loner who – as the group sing the words *'I wish I was special ... I don't belong here'* (the lyrics from *Creep*) – tries to join in a sweetly self-contained dance for two white-clad, angelic girls.

OVERLEAF: SCENES FROM *RIDE THE BEAST*

Other sections of Petronio's ballet suggest the tribal nature – the gangs, the minorities – of a hustling, vividly diverse metropolis. Cho's costumes help to define and separate these, using black for one group and bright rainbow colours for another. And though the basic shapes of his designs are simple, the details are intricately ornate: thickly braided ribbons that shower out into a flutter of individual strands, or else erupt, like the plumage of exotic birds. Whether the dancers are standing still or moving at Petronio's preferred high speed, the costumes are a clever way of leading our eye through the relationships, the interactions and the isolations that make the specially commissioned *Ride the Beast* such an exciting piece.

On page 138, Adam Blyde in hot pursuit of Claire Robertson. Page 139: Erik Cavallari (foreground) is caught in a demandingly athletic balance by Will Smith. Page 140: Louisa Hassell and Jarkko Lehmus come together like a living jigsaw.

ABOVE AND OPPOSITE: STEPHEN PETRONIO'S *MIDDLESEXGORGE*

'*Are you hot, are you hot, are you hot?*' demands the sound track, by punk-rock band Wire, and when Scottish Ballet took on Petronio's *MiddleSexGorge* for their debut appearance under Ashley Page in 2003, the dancers were sizzlingly hot. The revealing cutaway corsets worn by both sexes and the erotically charged, fierce moves made us look at Scottish Ballet in a new, jaw-dropping way. Exploring Petronio's movements here are: above, Jarkko Lehmus and Adam Blyde; opposite, Martina Forioso, Jarkko Lehmus, Paul Liburd, Luke Ahmet, Diana Loosmore and Adam Blyde.

PREVIOUS PAGES: PATRICIA HINES IN *32 CRYPTOGRAMS*

In Ashley Page's *32 Cryptograms* (page 141), a small number of dancers seem to defy mathematical possibilities with a constant flow of thrilling movement that suggests there are dozens of them lined up in the wings.

ABOVE AND OPPOSITE: ASHLEY PAGE'S *PENNIES FROM HEAVEN*
Classic crooning from the 1930s, classic ballet with a stylish twist in Ashley Page's *Pennies from Heaven*.
Above, Tama Barry and Luciana Ravizzi; opposite, Quenby Hersh.

OVERLEAF: *THE PUMP ROOM AND FEARFUL SYMMETRIES*
Paul Liburd and Sophie Martin in Ashley Page's *The Pump Room* (page 146). On the facing page,
Sophie Martin and Erik Cavallari in Page's *Fearful Symmetries*.

BELOW & OPPOSITE: GOING DUTCH

Claire Robertson and Erik Cavallari realise the crisp elegance but also the sexual tensions in Hans van Manen's *Two Ballets for Het*. 'Het' is the affectionate abbreviation for Dutch National Ballet, who had originally premiered these pieces.

OPPOSITE AND OVERLEAF: TRISHA BROWN'S *FOR MG: THE MOVIE*

In Scottish Ballet's Edinburgh International Festival programme in 2007, the company took some very unexpected steps... It performed Trisha Brown's *For MG: The Movie*. Made in 1991, with a soundscore by Alvin Curran, this piece is a reminder that Brown (who was then in her mid-fifties) had never reneged on the values that had badged her as a luminary of the New York post-modern avant-garde scene of the 1960s. Trisha Brown doesn't do story ballets. For her, dance is a physical abstraction. There is no deliberately contrived drama – none of those high-pitched fallings-in and fallings-out of sexual encounter – in her work. Instead, there is a deeply considered exploration of ideas: here those thoughts turn to what it actually means to perform. What influences an audience's perceptions of a space, of the bodies in that space, even their awareness (or not) of the passing of time.

Throughout the piece, a man stands absolutely still, facing upstage: we will only see his face when he joins in the final bow. Is he the still point in a turning world? We can, and probably do, make up our own stories, whatever Brown intends. We wonder why the Running Girl loops and runs endlessly in a ten-minute solo on the curiously derelict stage. We wonder why Curran's score, with its passages of haunting piano music, suddenly cuts to 'noises off': industrial clatter, street sounds, children's voices. And we wonder why nobody pays any attention to that standing man, clad like everyone else in a dusty-pink, almost flesh-coloured unitard.

But trying to analyse on a moment-to-moment basis gets you nowhere. Better, instead, to let your senses fall into the mesmerising flow of unbelievably slow bodies that appear and disappear, almost like magic, in the space. Respond to the poetic simplicity of movements that reiterate and build into sequences of precisely controlled, totally poised dance. And the title? MG is Michel Guy, a former French Minister of Culture who commissioned the work but died before it was made. 'The Movie' is a hint at how Brown's choreography is attempting the filmic trait of figures materialising before our eyes without us seeing, or indeed wondering, how they got there.

Opposite, Martina Forioso, running; overleaf, Vassilissa Levtonova and Nathalie Dupouy (both photos on pages 152–53); on pages 154, Sophie Laplane, Daniel Davidson and Tama Barry, with the Standing Man in the background. On page 155, Nathalie Dupouy and the Standing Man.

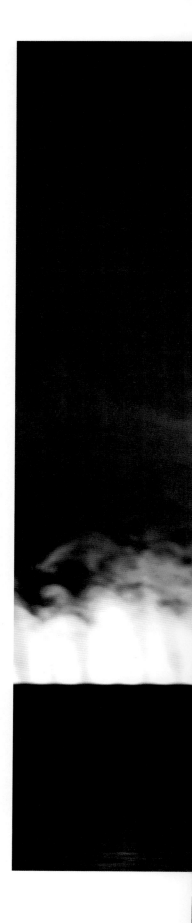

PREVIOUS PAGES AND RIGHT: WILLIAM FORSYTHE'S *ARTIFACT SUITE*
One of the greatest compliments a ballet company can receive is when an internationally acclaimed choreographer agrees to let them set foot in his work. In 2004, William Forsythe not only said 'yes' to Scottish Ballet taking on two sections from his *Artifact*, but he decided, after watching the dancers perform, that he would adapt and extend the two sections into a suite especially for the company.

The original, full-length *Artifact* – the first piece Forsythe made for Frankfurt Ballet when he became its director in 1984 – is rarely presented in its entirety now, probably because of the considerable resources needed to stage it with all the props, scenery and costuming in place. Scottish Ballet's *Artifact Suite*, however, dispenses with the period costumes, the moveable walls of the middle section set and the spoken text – often a kind of intellectual slanging match – that nodded in the direction of the essay by Michel Foucault that had been one of the starting points for Forsythe's choreography.

What then emerged was a suite of dances that retained the sense of dynamic theatricality, the virtuosic duets, the striking ensemble patternings, that had graced the original full-length work. The result was a stunning piece of 1980s radical experimention that had morphed into a timeless crowd-pleaser without dumbing down. Forsythe's flair for taking the familiar classical vocabulary and stretching, like a rubber band, set new challenges for Scottish Ballet's dancers. Hard work ensured they came to understand how Forsythe's choreography had a geometry, a rhythm of its own, as well as a different approach to weight transference and balance from, for instance, Balanchine.

And if you want to trigger audience memories of Scottish Ballet performing *Artifact Suite*, there's a sound cue to add to the following images. It's the THUD! of the fire curtain that falls repeatedly, like the sudden blink of a noisy camera shutter, only to rise again on a completely different stage picture... a new configuration of bodies, seamlessly, swiftly, silently achieved by the dancers.

On the previous pages, Eve Mutso demonstrates the arm movements that the whole company will then perform in crisply regimented unison. Opposite, Jarkko Lehmus and Claire Robertson in one of the technically testing duets that make audiences gasp and applaud.

Opposite and overleaf: William Forsythe's *Artifact Suite*

Costumes for *Artifact Suite* are basic: leotards, unitards, tights. No frill, no flounces to distract the eye from the lines drawn by the dancer's body. It's no coincidence that Forsythe has a passion for mathematics and architecture that informs the way he looks at how groups and individuals relate to one another and to the space around them. On a bare stage, in close-fitting lycra, there is nowhere to hide – no ornate costuming to hide behind. This choreography demands mental and physical stamina, acumen and rigour.

Opposite: Erik Cavallari, Patricia Hines and the company in Forsythe's *Artifact Suite*. Overleaf, the company line up in one of the striking formations that help make Forsythe's *Artifact Suite* a memorable masterpiece.

When dancers are learning new steps, they usually either count or rely on the music to help commit the moves to what is called 'muscle memory'. The score for *Artifact Suite* is a highly individual mix of sounds (chosen by Forsythe), with J.S. Bach and piano music by the late Eva Crossman-Hecht, and the mix doesn't make the dancers' task an easy one. Instead, the music acts as another layer in what you might call a discussion on structures, where visual counterpoint or oppositions create the kind of crackling energies and tensions Walt Whitman might have had in mind when he wrote: 'I sing the body electric'. Opposite, Erik Cavallari and Sophie Martin go with the electrifying flow of Forsythe's choreography.

Diana Loosmore's *Chasing Ghosts*

Peter Darrell's commitment to encouraging new talent was commemorated after his death by the Peter Darrell Choreographic Award. Scottish Ballet soloist Diana Loosmore was a winner in 2007. Her piece was performed at a Gala marking the 20th anniversary of Darrell's death. These images from *Chasing Ghosts* show Vassilissa Levtonova below and, with Eve Mutso and Erik Cavallari, opposite.

BELOW: LIGHT AND SHADOW, MOOD AND TEXTURE
The company in Krzysztof Pastor's *In Light and Shadow.*

Gregory Dean in *In Light and Shadow* (2006)

This wonderfully uplifting ballet established Krzysztof Pastor as a popular guest contributor to the Scottish Ballet's repertoire. Inspiration for *In Light and Shadow* came from various sources: Baroque dances, the paintings of artists like Vermeer, Rembrandt and La Tour, and the music of J.S. Bach. In each of these strands, Pastor saw the contrasts of mood and texture – the light and shadow – whether it was expressed in a gesture, a pigment, a shift in tempo or a key change. The resulting choreography is like a tapestry or a collage where the juxtaposition of styles, and of the thrillingly opulent design elements, lures an audience into a realm of witty, inventive dance that is touchingly alive with the joys and glooms of our own existence in light and shadow. Left: Gregory Dean, in golden-metallic costume, slips out of the shadows to catch the spotlight.

OPPOSITE: EVE MUTSO AND GREGORY DEAN IN *IN LIGHT AND SHADOW*
Krzysztov Pastor reworked some of his original choreography for this work to make the most of the technical diversity within Scottish Ballet. Opposite: Eve Mutso and Gregory Dean pause long enough for us to catch our breath at the lushly glinting folds of their costumes. Yards upon yards of sheeny material were fashioned into ravishing hide-and-peek costumes that fluttered and swirled – and flashed – as the dancers swooped across the stage, skirts (men too) flying out around them like molten metal. The effect was achingly magical, a perfect embodiment of the Baroque spirit that Pastor was celebrating.

Richard Alston's *Carmen* (2009)

When Richard Alston agreed to make a new, one-act *Carmen* for Scottish Ballet, it was the first time he had actually set out to choreograph a storytelling ballet. Known worldwide as a dance-maker at the forefront of the UK contemporary scene, Alston had also decided that he would seize the opportunity of working with classically trained dancers to explore how his own movement vocabulary might mesh and cross over with theirs. So pointe-shoes were in. But castanets and phoney flamenco were definitely out.

Alston's Carmen would have a fierce, independent spirit, but she would not be the kind of clichéd 'rose between the teeth' femme fatale that so often flounces through opera productions and some other ballets. Instead, Alston pored over Prosper Merimée's short novel and came away with a strong sense of three young people – Carmen, Don José and Escamillo – whose lives briefly, and fatefully, intertwine. Fate would enter the action, in the symbolic figure of the fortune teller, and it would sound throughout the piece in the percussive clangour of Rodin Schedrin's *Carmen Suite*, a vivid reduction of the Bizet score that uses only strings and percussion and lasts for under an hour.

On the previous pages In Alston's ballet, Martina Forioso (Carmen) is ready to catch the eye of any passing soldier she fancies. William Smith, as the toreador Escamillo, is ready to engage with danger, whether in the bull-ring or the boudoir.

Left: Carmen may be in handcuffs, but the glint in her eye reveals she already knows that hapless, inexperienced Don José (Daniel Davidson) will be putty in her hands. Overleaf: he didn't want her to die, he just wanted her back... Don José looks on in horror at Carmen's outstretched body.

CLAIRE ROBERTSON AND ADAM BLYDE IN FREDERICK ASHTON'S *SCÈNES DE BALLET*
When Stravinsky wrote the music for *Scènes de Ballet* in the 1940s he wasn't composing with any plot or literary meaning in mind. He was simply intent on making music for dance. Sir Frederick Ashton's choreography answers that remit with characteristic brilliance. This is classical ballet that celebrates the art form.

CHRONOLOGY

1969

MAY (WITH SCOTTISH OPERA)
The Trojans
Choreographer: Laverne Meyer
Composer: Hector Berlioz
PERFORMED IN GLASGOW

SPRING
Breakaway
Choreographer: Gillian Lynne
Composer: Barry Booth
Cage of God
Choreographer: Jack Carter
Composer: Alan Rawsthorne
Ephemeron
Choreographer: Peter Darrell
Composer: Milhaud
PERFORMED IN GLASGOW

AUTUMN
La Ventana
Choreographer: August Bournonville
Composer: Hans Christian Lumbye
Spectrum
Choreographer: Clover Roope
Composer: Malcolm Williamson
The Lesson
Choreographer: Flemming Flindt
Composer: Georges Delerue
Frontier
Choreographer: John Neumeier
Composer: Sir Arthur Bliss
PERFORMED IN PERTH

WINTER
Beauty & the Beast
Choreographer: Peter Darrell
Composer: Thea Musgrave
PERFORMED IN LONDON & EDINBURGH

1970

BALLET AT THE CLOSE
New works by the following members of the company:
Choreographer: Kenn Wells
Composer: Villa-Lobos
Choreographer: Tatsuo Sakai
Composer: Traditional Japanese
Choreographer: Domy Reiter
Composer: Bach
Choreographer: Gernot Petzold
Composer: William Kraft
Choreographer: Ashley Killar
Composer: Maricio Kagel
Choreographer: Brian Burn
Composer: Jagger / Richards / Wyman
PERFORMED IN GLASGOW

SPRING/SUMMER
Points of Contact
Choreographer: Clover Roope
Composer: Bob Woolford
Dances from William Tell
Choreographer: August Bournonville
Composer: Gioachino Rossini
Herodias
Choreographer: Peter Darrell
Composer: Adolphe Adam
PERFORMED IN LONDON
Giselle
Choreographer: Peter Darrell/ Jean Corelli/Jules Perrot
Composer: Hindemith
PERFORMED IN ABERDEEN

1970–1972

PLOYS PROGRAMME
Journey
Choreographer: Ashley Killar
Composer: Leos Janácek
Maze
Choreographer: Gernot Petzold
Composer: Claude Debussy / Matsudaira / Varese
Sleepers
Choreographer: Stuart Hopps
Whirlpool
Choreographer: Peter Cazalet
Composer: Takemitsu
Lovedu
Choreographer: Kenn Wells
Composer: Leonard Salzedo
Landscape
Choreographers: Peter Logan/ Karl Brown
Composer: Brian Hodgson
PERFORMED IN EDINBURGH & LONDON

1971

SCOTTISH ARTS COUNCIL TOUR
Peepshow
Choreographer: Walter Gore
Composer: Jean Françaix
Four Portraits
Choreographer: Peter Darrell
Composer: Sergei Prokofiev
PERFORMED IN CALLANDER

1971–72

La Ventana
Choreographer: August Bournonville
Composer: Hans Christian Lumbye
PERFORMED IN GLASGOW, EDINBURGH, ABERDEEN & PERTH
Arriving Bellevue Sunday
Choreographer: Ashley Killar
Composer: Leos Janácek
PERFORMED IN OXFORD, WOLVERHAMPTON & NORWICH
La Fête Étrange
Choreographer: Andrée Howard
Composer: Gabriel Fauré
PERFORMED IN MANCHESTER, STIRLING, LIVERPOOL & BILLINGHAM
Beauty and the Beast
Choreographer: Peter Darrell
Composer: Thea Musgrave
PERFORMED IN SWANSEA, BLACKPOOL, SUNDERLAND & ZURICH.
Giselle
Choreographer: Peter Darrell / Jean Corelli / Jules Perrot
Composer: Hindemith

1972

CHOREOGRAPHIC WORKSHOPS
Iseult
Choreographer: Gernot Petzold
Composer: Boris Blacher
Transfigured
Choreographer: Nicholas Carroll
Composer: Schoenberg
PERFORMED IN GLASGOW

WINTER
Dances from William Tell
Choreographer: August Bournonville
Composer: Gioachino Rossini
Street Games
Choreographer: Walter Gore
Composer: Jacques Ibert
An Clo Mor (The Big Cloth)
Choreographer: Stuart Hopps
Composer: Traditional Gaelic

1972

Journey
Choreographer: Ashley Killar
Composer: Leos Janácek
PERFORMED IN GLASGOW & EDINBURGH

SPRING
Tales of Hoffmann
Choreographer: Peter Darrell
Composer: Jacques Offenbach / Arr. Lanchberry
Street Games
Choreographer: Walter Gore
Composer: Jacques Ibert
La Fête Étrange
Choreographer: Andrée Howard
Composer: Gabriel Fauré
The Lesson
Choreographer: Flemming Flindt
Composer: Georges Delerue
PERFORMED IN EDINBURGH, GLASGOW, ABERDEEN, HULL & CARDIFF

CHOREOGRAPHIC WORKSHOPS
Reverence to Rameau
Choreographer: Harold King
Composer: Rameau
Rachmaninov Pas de Six
Choreographer: James Supervia
Composer: Rachmaninov
Landscape
Choreographer: Peter Logan / Karl Brown
Composer: Brian Hodgson
Vivaldi + 4
Choreographer: Brian Burn
Composer: Vivaldi
Interval
Choreographer: Cecelia MacFarlane
Composer: Bob Downes
Scope
Choreographer: Gernot Petzold
Composer: Scriabin
Good Ol' Sambo
Choreographer: Anthony West
Composer: George Gershwin
The Hollow Mask
Choreographer: Stephen Lansley
Composer: Bartók / Lake / Palmer
PERFORMED IN GLASGOW

TANGENTS TOUR
Positively the Last Final Farewell Performance
Choreographer: Stuart Hopps
Composer: Glenn Miller
Balkan Sobranie
Choreographer: Richard Alston
Composer: Stravinsky / Francaix / Fukushimo
Some Bright Star
Choreographer: Peter Cazalet
Composer: Pink Floyd / Malec / Tonto's Band
Forme et Ligne
Choreographer: Maurice Béjart
Composer: Pierre Henry
PERFORMED IN GLASGOW & EDINBURGH

OCHTERTYRE FESTIVAL
An Clo Mor (The Big Cloth)
Choreographer: Stuart Hopps
Composer: Traditional Gaelic
Tales of Hoffmann (pas de trois - prologue)
Choreographer: Peter Darrell
Composer: Jacques Offenbach / Arr. Lanchberry

1972–1973

The Nutcracker (pas de deux)
Choreographer: Peter Darrell / Lev Ivanov
Composer: Tchaikovsky
Giselle (pas de deux)
Choreographer: Lev Ivanov
Composer: Adolphe Adam
Street Games
Choreographer: Walter Gore
Composer: Jacques Ibert
La Ventana (pas de trois)
Choreographer: August Bournonville
Composer: Hans Christian Lumbye
PERFORMED IN CRIEFF

PLOYS TOUR
Lovedu (The People of the Rain Queen)
Choreographer: Kenn Wells
Composer: Leonard Salzedo
Sleepers
Choreographer: Stuart Hopps
Whirlpool
Choreographer: Peter Cazalet
Composer: Takemitsu
Match for 3 Players
Choreographer: Ashley Killar
Composer: Mauricio Kagel
Maze
Choreographer: Gernot Petzold
Composer: Debussy / Matsudaira / Varese
PERFORMED IN LONDON, GLASGOW, EDINBURGH & NEWCASTLE

AUTUMN
The Nutcracker (Act II)
Choreographer: Peter Darrell / Lev Ivanov
Composer: Tchaikovsky (Salzedo)
Sonate à Trois
Choreographer: Maurice Béjart
Composer: Béla Bartók
Cage of God
Choreographer: Jack Carter
Composer: Alan Rawsthorne
Light Fantastic
Choreographer: Walter Gore
Composer: Emmanuel Chabrier
Tales of Hoffmann
Choreographer: Peter Darrell
Composer: Jacques Offenbach / Arr. Lanchberry
PERFORMED IN EDINBURGH, GLASGOW, STIRLING, NEWCASTLE, BILLINGHAM & ABERDEEN

1973

FANFARE FOR EUROPE
Tango Chikane
Choreographer: Flemming Flindt
Composer: Tango / Jealousy
The Nutcracker (pas de deux)
Choreographer: Peter Darrell / Lev Ivanov
Composer: Tchaikovsky
Scorpius
Choreographer: Peter Darrell
Composer: Thea Musgrave
Valse Excentrique
Choreographer: Kenneth MacMillan
Composer: Jacques Ibert
Flower Festival at Genzano (pas de deux)
Choreographer: August Bournonville
Composer: Helsted / Paulli

1973

La Ventana
Choreographer: August Bournonville
Composer: Hans Christian Lumbye
Street Games
Choreographer: Walter Gore
Composer: Jacques Ibert
PERFORMED IN GLASGOW

BALLET FOR SCOTLAND TOUR
Scarlatti and Friends
Choreographer: André Prokovsky
Composer: Scarlatti / Scarlatti / Fiorenza
Soirée Musicale
Choreographer: Antony Tudor
Composer: Gioachino Rossini
The Nutcracker (pas de deux)
Choreographer: Peter Darrell / Lev Ivanov
Composer: Tchaikovsky
Peepshow
Choreographer: Walter Gore
Composer: Jean Françaix
Some Bright Star
Choreographer: Peter Cazalet
Composer: Pink Floyd / Malec / Tonto's Band
Flower Festival at Genzano (pas de deux)
Choreographer: August Bournonville
Composer: Helsted / Paulli
An Clo Mor (The Big Cloth)
Choreographer: Stuart Hopps
Composer: Traditional Gaelic
Beauty and the Beast
Choreographer: John Cranko
Composer: Maurice Ravel
PERFORMED IN DUNDEE, PRESTWICK, AIRDRIE, GREENOCK, DUNS, PRESTONPANS, ANSTRUTHER, ABERDOUR, KILMARNOCK, DUMFRIES, STRATHAVEN, BEITH, TROON & KIRKUDBRIGHT

SPRING TOUR
Le Carnaval
Choreographer: Mikhail Fokine
Composer: Robert Schumann
Ways of Saying Bye Bye
Choreographer: Toer van Schayk
Composer: Purcell / Poptie / Pickett / Harbach / Hoschna
The Nutcracker (Act II)
Choreographer: Peter Darrell / Lev Ivanov
Composer: Tchaikovsky
Giselle
Choreographer: Peter Darrell / Jean Corelli / Jules Perrot
Composer: Adolphe Adam
PERFORMED IN BRADFORD, EDINBURGH, GLASGOW, BIRMINGHAM, CARDIFF, SWANSEA & ABERDEEN

BALLET AT THE GATEWAY
Three Dances to Japanese Music
Choreographer: Jack Carter
Composer: Traditional Japanese
Valse Excentrique
Choreographer: Kenneth MacMillan
Composer: Jacques Ibert
Scorpius
Choreographer: Peter Darrell
Composer: Thea Musgrave
Jeux
Choreographer: Peter Darrell
Composer: Claude Debussy

1973–1974

Sonate à Trois
Choreographer: Maurice Béjart
Composer: Béla Bartók
Soirée Musicale
Choreographer: Antony Tudor
Composer: Gioachino Rossini /
Arr. Britten
PERFORMED IN EDINBURGH

AUTUMN
Three Dances to Japanese Music
Choreographer: Jack Carter
Composer: Traditional Japanese
Flower Festival at Genzano
(pas de deux)
Choreographer: August Bournonville
Composer: Helsted / Paulli
Ephemeron
Choreographer: Peter Darrell
Composer: Darius Milhaud
Embers of Glencoe
Choreographer: Walter Gore
Composer: Thomas Wilson
La Sylphide
Choreographer: August Bournonville
Composer: Herman Lovenskjold
Ways of Saying Bye Bye
Choreographer: Toer van Schayk
Composer: Purcell / Poptie /
Pickett / Harbach / Hoschna
PERFORMED IN NOTTINGHAM,
GLASGOW, STIRLING, ABERDEEN,
EDINBURGH, BRADFORD,
SUNDERLAND & BILLINGHAM

WINTER 1973/1974
The Nutcracker
Choreographer: Peter Darrell /
Lev Ivanov
Composer: Tchaikovsky
PERFORMED IN EDINBURGH

1974
AUSTRALASIAN TOUR WITH
MARGOT FONTEYN AND IVAN NAGY
Swan Lake (Act II)
Choreographer: Lev Ivanov
Composer: Tchaikovsky
Flower Festival at Genzano
(pas de deux)
Choreographer: August Bournonville
Composer: Helsted / Paulli
Romeo & Juliet (pas de deux)
Choreographer: George Skibine
Composer: Hector Berlioz
Tales of Hoffmann (Act II)
Choreographer: Peter Darrell
Composer: Jacques Offenbach /
Arr. Lanchberry
Sonate à Trois
Choreographer: Maurice Béjart
Composer: Béla Bartók
La Ventana
Choreographer: August Bournonville
Composer: Hans Christian Lumbye
The Nutcracker (Act II)
Choreographer: Peter Darrell /
Lev Ivanov
Composer: Tchaikovsky
Three Dances to Japanese Music
Choreographer: Jack Carter
Composer: Traditional Japanese
La Sylphide
Choreographer: August Bournonville
Composer: Hermann Lovenskjold
PERFORMED IN PERTH,
MELBOURNE, ADELAIDE & SYDNEY

1974–1975

(AUSTRALIA); WELLINGTON
& DUNEDIN (NEW ZEALAND)

SUMMER
Grand Pas Gitane
Choreographer: Peter Darrell
Composer: Camille Saint-Saëns
La Sylphide (pas de deux)
Choreographer: August Bournonville
Composer: Hermann Lovenskjold
The Nutcracker (pas de deux)
Choreographer: Peter Darrell /
Lev Ivanov
Composer: Tchaikovsky
Tales of Hoffmann (pas de deux)
Choreographer: Peter Darrell
Composer: Jacques Offenbach /
Arr. Lanchberry
PERFORMED IN CRIEFF

AUTUMN TOUR
La Ventana
Choreographer: August Bournonville
Composer: Hans Christian Lumbye
La Sylphide
Choreographer: August Bournonville
Composer: Hermann Lovenskjold
Tales of Hoffmann
Choreographer: Peter Darrell
Composer: Jacques Offenbach /
Arr. Lanchberry
PERFORMED IN HULL, NOTTINGHAM,
STIRLING, GLASGOW,
LIVERPOOL & EDINBURGH

GALA PERFORMANCE W. MARGOT
FONTEYN AND IVAN NAGY
Love Duet from Romeo & Juliet
Choreographer: George Skibine
Composer: Hector Berlioz
The Dancing Floor
Choreographer: Jack Carter
Composer: Morton Subotnik
Swan Lake (pas de deux)
Choreographer: Lev Ivanov
Composer: Tchaikovsky
Valse Excentrique
Choreographer: Kenneth MacMillan
Composer: Jacques Ibert
Intimate Pages
Choreographer: Harold King
Composer: Leos Janácek
La Ventana
Choreographer: August Bournonville
Composer: Hans Christian Lumbye
PERFORMED IN GLASGOW

1974/1975 CHRISTMAS SEASON
The Nutcracker
Choreographer: Peter Darrell /
Lev Ivanov
Composer: Tchaikovsky
PERFORMED IN ABERDEEN

1975
BALLET FOR SCOTLAND TOUR
Scarlatti and Friends
Choreographer: André Prokovsky
Composer: Scarlatti /
Scarlatti / Fiorenza
Triptych: O Caritas
Choreographer: Peter Darrell
Composer: Toumazi /
Taylor / Stevens
The Nutcracker (pas de deux)
Choreographer: Peter Darrell /
Lev Ivanov
Composer: Tchaikovsky

1975

Street Games
Choreographer: Walter Gore
Composer: Jacques Ibert
PERFORMED IN DUNS, CUMBERNAULD,
TROON, DUMBARTON, PAISLEY,
GREENOCK, BRORA, INVERGORDON,
ELGIN, KEITH, KINGUSSIE & DUMFRIES

SCOTTISH THEATRES TOUR
Offenbach Variations
Composer: Jacques Offenbach
Three Dances to Japanese Music
Choreographer: Jack Carter
Composer: Traditional Japanese
Flower Festival at Genzano
(pas de deux)
Choreographer: August Bournonville
Composer: Helsted / Paulli
Intimate Pages
Choreographer: Harold King
Composer: Leos Janácek
PERFORMED IN DUNDEE & KIRKCALDY

SPRING TOUR
Flower Festival at Genzano
(pas de deux)
Choreographer: August Bournonville
Composer: Helsted / Paulli
Three Dances to Japanese Music
Choreographer: Jack Carter
Composer: Traditional Japanese
La Fête Étrange
Choreographer: Andrée Howard
Composer: Gabriel Fauré
Giselle
Choreographer: Peter Darrell /
Jean Corelli / Jules Perrot
Composer: Adolphe Adam
Paquita
Choreographer: Marius Petipa
Composer: Minkus
The Dancing Floor
Choreographer: Jack Carter
Composer: Morton Subotnik
PERFORMED IN EDINBURGH,
LIVERPOOL, BATH, NEWCASTLE,
HULL, GLASGOW, PERTH & ABERDEEN

GALA PERFORMANCE
Pas de Quatre
Choreographer: Anton Dolin
Composer: Cesare Pugni
Paquita
Choreographer: Marius Petipa
Composer: Minkus
Spring Waters
Choreographer: Asaf Messerer
Composer: Rachmaninov
Forme et Ligne
Choreographer: Maurice Béjart
Composer: Pierre Henry
O Caritas
Choreographer: Peter Darrell
Composer: Toumazi /
Taylor / Stevens
Taras Bulba
Choreographer: Boris Feuster
Composer: Vasily Solovyov-Syedoy
La Fête Étrange
Choreographer: Andrée Howard
Composer: Gabriel Fauré
PERFORMED IN GLASGOW

SUMMER
The Dancing Floor
Choreographer: Jack Carter
Composer: Morton Subotnik

1975

La Sylphide
Choreographer: August Bournonville
Composer: Hermann Lovenskjold
The Nutcracker
Choreographer: Peter Darrell /
Lev Ivanov
Composer: Tchaikovsky
Giselle
Choreographer: Peter Darrell /
Jean Corelli / Jules Perrot
Composer: Adolphe Adam
PERFORMED IN EDINBURGH

INTERNATIONAL FESTIVAL OF DANCE
The Lesson
Choreographer: Flemming Flindt
Composer: Georges Delerue
Moment
Choreographer: Murray Louis
Composer: Maurice Ravel
Three Dances to Japanese Music
Choreographer: Jack Carter
Composer: Traditional Japanese
Flower Festival at Genzano
(pas de deux)
Choreographer: August Bournonville
Composer: Helsted / Paulli
Variations for Four
Choreographer: Anton Dolin
Composer: Marguerite Keogh
Paquita
Choreographer: Marius Petipa
Composer: Minkus
Sonate à Trois
Choreographer: Maurice Béjart
Composer: Béla Bartók
La Sylphide
Choreographer: August Bournonville
Composer: Hermann Lovenskjold
PERFORMED IN MADRID

INTERNATIONAL FESTIVAL
OF BALLET
Three Dances to Japanese Music
Choreographer: Jack Carter
Composer: Traditional Japanese
La Sylphide
Choreographer: August Bournonville
Composer: Hermann Lovenskjold
Tales of Hoffmann
Choreographer: Peter Darrell
Composer: Jacques Offenbach /
Arr. Lanchberry
PERFORMED IN BARCELONA (SPAIN)

AUTUMN TOUR
The Lesson
Choreographer: Flemming Flindt
Composer: Georges Delerue
Variations for Four
Choreographer: Anton Dolin
Composer: Marguerite Keogh
Pas de Quatre
Choreographer: Anton Dolin
Composer: Cesare Pugni
Grande Pas Gitane
Choreographer: Peter Darrell
Composer: Camille Saint-Saëns
Le Carnaval
Choreographer: Mikhail Fokine
Composer: Robert Schumann
The Scarlet Pastorale
Choreographer: Peter Darrell
Composer: Frank Martin
Le Corsaire (pas de deux)
Choreographer: Marius Petipa
Composer: Riccardo Drigo

1975–1976

O Caritas
Choreographer: Peter Darrell
Composer: Toumazi /
Taylor / Stevens
Intimate Pages
Choreographer: Harold King
Composer: Leos Janácek
Harlequinade
Choreographer: Marius Petipa/
John Gilpin
Composer: Riccardo Drigo
PERFORMED IN EDINBURGH,
GLASGOW, ABERDEEN & NORWICH

BALLET FOR SCOTLAND TOUR
Sonate à Trois
Choreographer: Maurice Béjart
Composer: Béla Bartók
Pas de Quatre
Choreographer: Anton Dolin
Composer: Cesare Pugni
La Ventana
Choreographer: August Bournonville
Composer: Hans Christian Lumbye
Flower Festival at Genzano
(pas de deux)
Choreographer: August Bournonville
Composer: Edvard Helsted
Beauty and the Beast
Choreographer: Peter Darrell
Composer: Musgrave
PERFORMED IN DUNFERMLINE, LARGS,
DUNOON, KILMARNOCK, ARBROATH,
NAIRN, DUMBARTON & MUSSELBURGH

1975 / 1976 CHRISTMAS SEASON
The Nutcracker
Choreographer: Peter Darrell /
Lev Ivanov
Composer: Tchaikovsky
PERFORMED IN GLASGOW

1976
SPRING
La Fête Étrange
Choreographer: Andrée Howard
Composer: Gabriel Fauré
Paquita
Choreographer: Marius Petipa
Composer: Minkus
La Sylphide
Choreographer: August Bournonville
Composer: Hermann Lovenskjold
La Ventana
Choreographer: August Bournonville
Composer: Hans Christian Lumbye
Giselle
Choreographer: Peter Darrell /
Jean Corelli / Jules Perrot
Composer: Adolphe Adam
Tales of Hoffmann
Choreographer: Peter Darrell
Composer: Jacques Offenbach/
Arr. Lanchberry
Mary Queen of Scots
Choreographer: Peter Darrell
Composer: John McCabe
The Lesson
Choreographer: Flemming Flindt
Composer: Georges Delerue
Jeux
Choreographer: Peter Darrell
Composer: Claude Debussy
O Caritas
Choreographer: Peter Darrell
Composer: Toumazi /
Taylor / Stevens

1976

Le Carnaval
Choreographer: Mikhail Fokine
Composer: Robert Schumann
Three Dances to Japanese Music
Choreographer: Jack Carter
Composer: Traditional Japanese
Pas de Quatre
Choreographer: Anton Dolin
Composer: Cesare Pugni
Performed in Glasgow

Sadler's Wells Season
Royal gala performance with
Margot Fonteyn & Anthony Dowell
The Scarlet Pastorale
Choreographer: Peter Darrell
Composer: Frank Martin
Mary Queen of Scots
Choreographer: Peter Darrell
Composer: John McCabe
Tales of Hoffmann
Choreographer: Peter Darrell
Composer: Jacques Offenbach /
Arr. Lanchberry
Giselle
Choreographer: Peter Darrell /
Jean Corelli / Jules Perrot
Composer: Adolphe Adam
La Fête Étrange
Choreographer: Andrée Howard
Composer: Gabriel Fauré
Belong
Choreographer: Norbert Vesak
Composer: Syrinx
Paquita
Choreographer: Marius Petipa
Composer: Minkus
Pas de Quatre
Choreographer: Anton Dolin
Composer: Cesare Pugni
O Caritas
Choreographer: Peter Darrell
Composer: Toumazi /
Taylor / Stevens
The Nutcracker (Act II)
Choreographer: Peter Darrell /
Lev Ivanov
Composer: Tchaikovsky
Three Dances to Japanese Music
Choreographer: Jack Carter
Composer: Traditional Japanese
La Ventana
Choreographer: August Bournonville
Composer: Hans Christian Lumbye
Tales of Hoffmann
Choreographer: Peter Darrell
Composer: Jacques Offenbach /
Arr. Lanchberry
Mary Queen of Scots
Choreographer: Peter Darrell
Composer: John McCabe
Le Carnaval
Choreographer: Mikhail Fokine
Composer: Robert Schumann
Jeux
Choreographer: Peter Darrell
Composer: Claude Debussy
The Lesson
Choreographer: Flemming Flindt
Composer: Georges Delerue
La Sylphide
Choreographer: August Bournonville
Composer: Hermann Lovenskjold
Performed in London

1976

Spring Tour
Mary Queen of Scots
Choreographer: Peter Darrell
Composer: John McCabe
Tales of Hoffmann
Choreographer: Peter Darrell
Composer: Jacques Offenbach /
Arr. Lanchberry
La Ventana
Choreographer: August Bournonville
Composer: Hans Christian Lumbye
Three Dances to Japanese Music
Choreographer: Jack Carter
Composer: Traditional Japanese
The Nutcracker (Act II)
Choreographer: Peter Darrell /
Lev Ivanov
Composer: Tchaikovsky
O Caritas
Choreographer: Peter Darrell
Composer: Toumazi /
Taylor / Stevens
Pas de Quatre
Choreographer: Anton Dolin
Composer: Cesare Pugni
Giselle
Choreographer: Peter Darrell /
Jean Corelli / Jules Perrot
Composer: Adolphe Adam
Performed in Hull, Edinburgh,
Liverpool, Inverness, Stirling,
Kirkcaldy, Perth & Aberdeen

Nureyev Festival
The Lesson
Choreographer: Flemming Flindt
Composer: Georges Delerue
La Sylphide
Choreographer: August Bournonville
Composer: Hermann Lovenskjold
Moment
Choreographer: Murray Louis
Composer: Maurice Ravel
Three Dances to Japanese Music
Choreographer: Jack Carter
Composer: Traditional Japanese
Performed in London

Summer
The Scarlet Pastorale
Choreographer: Peter Darrell
Composer: Frank Martin
Belong
Choreographer: Norbert Vesak
Composer: Syrinx
Othello
Choreographer: Peter Darrell
Composer: Franz Liszt
Paquita
Choreographer: Marius Petipa
Composer: Minkus
Mary Queen of Scots
Choreographer: Peter Darrell
Composer: John McCabe
Giselle
Choreographer: Peter Darrell /
Jean Corelli / Jules Perrot
Composer: Adolphe Adam
Tales of Hoffmann
Choreographer: Peter Darrell
Composer: Jacques Offenbach /
Arr. Lanchberry
Performed in Edinburgh, Aberdeen
& Glasgow

1976–1977

Ballet for Scotland Tour
Othello
Choreographer: Peter Darrell
Composer: Franz Liszt
Harlequinade
Choreographer: Marius Petipa /
Gilpin
Composer: Riccardo Drigo
O Caritas
Choreographer: Peter Darrell
Composer: Toumazi /
Taylor / Stevens
Belong
Choreographer: Norbert Vesak
Composer: Syrinx
Soirée Musicale
Choreographer: Antony Tudor
Composer: Gioachino Rossini /
Arr. Britten
Performed in Kilmarnock, Penicuik,
Dalkeith, Dumfries, Oban,
Campbeltown, Tawick, Dumbarton,
Dunoon, Paisley, Ashington,
Arbroath, Cumbernauld,
Helensburgh, Largs, Prestwick,
Leven, Falkirk, Musselburgh,
Thurso, Brora, Nairn & Aboyne

Christmas 1976/1977
The Nutcracker
Choreographer: Peter Darrell /
Lev Ivanov
Composer: Tchaikovsky
Performed in Edinburgh & Glasgow

1977
Nureyev Festival
Three Dances to Japanese Music
Choreographer: Jack Carter
Composer: Traditional Japanese
La Sylphide
Choreographer: August Bournonville
Composer: Hermann Lovenskjold
Giselle
Choreographer: Peter Darrell /
Jean Corelli / Jules Perrot
Composer: Adolphe Adam
Performed in Paris (France)

Spring Tour
Three Dances to Japanese Music
Choreographer: Jack Carter
Composer: Traditional Japanese
La Sylphide
Choreographer: August Bournonville
Composer: Hermann Lovenskjold
Swan Lake
Choreographer: Marius Petipa /
Lev Ivanov
Composer: Tchaikovsky
Performed in Wolverhampton,
Southsea, Glasgow, Edinburgh,
Aberdeen, Inverness & Hull

Joint Season with
Scottish Opera
Giselle
Choreographer: Peter Darrell /
Jean Corelli / Jules Perrot
Composer: Adolphe Adam
The Nutcracker
Choreographer: Peter Darrell /
Lev Ivanov
Composer: Tchaikovsky
Performed in Edinburgh

1977

Edinburgh Festival
The Scarlet Pastorale
Choreographer: Peter Darrell
Composer: Frank Martin
Don Quixote (pas de deux)
Choreographer: Marius Petipa
Composer: Minkus
Othello
Choreographer: Peter Darrell
Composer: Franz Liszt
Les Sylphides
Choreographer: Mikhail Fokine
Composer: Frédéric Chopin
Three Dances to Japanese Music
Choreographer: Jack Carter
Composer: Traditional Japanese
La Sylphide
Choreographer: August Bournonville
Composer: Hermann Lovenskjold

Spanish Tour
Three Dances to Japanese Music
Choreographer: Jack Carter
Composer: Traditional Japanese
Don Quixote (pas de deux)
Choreographer: Marius Petipa
Composer: Minkus
Cage of God
Choreographer: Jack Carter
Composer: Alan Rawsthorne
Spartacus (pas de deux)
Choreographer: Yuri Grigorovitch
Composer: Katchaturian
La Ventana
Choreographer: August Bournonville
Composer: Hans Christian Lumbye
Othello
Choreographer: Peter Darrell
Composer: Franz Liszt
Swan Lake (pas de deux)
Choreographer: Lev Ivanov
Composer: Tchaikovsky
O Caritas
Choreographer: Peter Darrell
Composer: Toumazi /
Taylor / Stevens
Spring Waters (pas de deux)
Choreographer: Asaf Messerer
Composer: Rachmaninov
Les Sylphides
Choreographer: Mikhail Fokine
Composer: Frédéric Chopin
Performed in St. Jean de Luz,
San Sebastian & Biarritz (Spain)

Ballet for Scotland Tour
Vespri
Choreographer: André Prokovsky
Composer: Verdi
Swan Lake (pas de deux)
Choreographer: Lev Ivanov
Composer: Tchaikovsky
Cage of God
Choreographer: Jack Carter
Composer: Alan Rawsthorne
*Flower Festival at Genzano
(pas de deux)*
Choreographer: August Bournonville
Composer: Edvard Helsted
Don Quixote (pas de deux)
Choreographer: Marius Petipa
Composer: Minkus
Suite from Les Sylphides
Choreographer: Mikhail Fokine
Composer: Frédéric Chopin
Performed in Dalkeith, Largs,

1977–1978

Rothesay, Hawick, Ashington,
St Andrews, Penicuik, Dumbarton,
Erskine, Troon, Dunoon, Kelso,
Campbeltown, Kirkcaldy,
Newcastle, Dumfries, Aboyne,
Nairn, Brora, Fort William,
Oban, Falkirk, Cumbernauld,
Musselburgh & Dundee

Christmas 1977/1978
the Nutcracker
The Nutcracker
Choreographer: Peter Darrell /
Lev Ivanov
Composer: Tchaikovsky
Performed in Aberdeen,
Inverness & Glasgow

1978
New Work Season
6 Easy Pieces
Choreographer: Linden Currey
Composer: Jean-Michel Jarre
Flower Walk
Choreographer: Christopher Long
Composer: Scott Joplin
Lightforce
Choreographer: Susan Cooper
Composer: Earley
Conflict
Choreographer: Judy Mohekey
Composer: Ehrlich
Night on the Steppes
Choreographer: Christopher
Blagdon / Serge Julien
Composer: Kaberalevsky
Three Songs
Choreographer: William Bowen
Composer: Gustav Mahler
Memories of Nina
Choreographer: Roy
Campbell-Moore
Composer: Shostakovitch
*In a White Room
with Black Curtains*
Choreographer: Anna McCartney
Composer: Cream
Autumn
Choreographer: Gordon Aitken
Composer: Glaszounov
Changing Music
Choreographer: Peter Royston
Composer: Focus / Debussy /
Shostakovitch
Everybody's a Star
Choreographer: Peter Royston
Composer: Led Zeppelin
One Minus Two
Choreographer: Roy
Campbell-Moore
Composer: Robert Schumann
Performed in Glasgow

Spring Season
Vespri
Choreographer: André Prokovsky
Composer: Verdi
Othello
Choreographer: Peter Darrell
Composer: Franz Liszt
Jeux/Belong
Choreographer: Peter Darrell /
Norbert Versak
Composer: Debussy / Syrinx
Les Sylphides
Choreographer: Mikhail Fokine

1978

Composer: Frédéric Chopin
Swan Lake
Choreographer: Marius Petipa / Lev Ivanov
Composer: Tchaikovsky
PERFORMED IN ABERDEEN, CARDIFF, HULL, SUNDERLAND, DARLINGTON, PERTH, GLASGOW, STIRLING, EDINBURGH & INVERNESS

SUMMER
Tales of Hoffmann
Choreographer: Peter Darrell
Composer: Jacques Offenbach
Vespri
Choreographer: André Prokovsky
Composer: Verdi
Dancing Floor
Choreographer: Jack Carter
Composer: Morton Subotnik
Napoli
Choreographer: August Bournonville
Composer: Gade / Helsted / Pauli / Lumbye
Swan Lake (Act II)
Choreographer: Lev Ivanov
Composer: Tchaikovsky
PERFORMED IN EDINBURGH & GLASGOW

SANTANDER SEASON
Vespri
Choreographer: André Prokovsky
Composer: Giuseppe Verdi
Walpurgis Night
Choreographer: Galina Samsova
Composer: Gounod
Dancing Floor
Choreographer: Jack Carter
Composer: Morton Subotnik
Swan Lake (Act II)
Choreographer: Lev Ivanov
Composer: Tchaikovsky
Les Sylphides
Choreographer: Mikhail Fokine
Composer: Frédéric Chopin
Three Dances to Japanese Music
Choreographer: Jack Carter
Composer: Traditional Japanese
Sleeping Beauty (pas de deux)
Choreographer: Marius Petipa
Composer: Tchaikovsky
Othello
Choreographer: Peter Darrell
Composer: Franz Liszt
PERFORMED IN SANTANDER (SPAIN)

BALLET FOR SCOTLAND
Dances from Napoli
Choreographer: August Bournonville
Composer: Gade / Helsted / Pauli / Lumbye
Beauty and the Beast
Choreographer: Peter Darrell
Composer: Musgrave
Five Rückert Songs
Choreographer: Peter Darrell
Composer: Gustav Mahler
Naila
Choreographer: Gordon Aitken
Composer: Leo Delibes
PERFORMED IN DUNDEE, STIRLING, CAMPBELTOWN, OBAN, ABOYNE, DUMFRIES, GALASHIELS, KELSO, HAWICK, KIRKCALDY, ELGIN, FORT WILLIAM, NAIRN, BRORA, DUMBARTON, LARGS, ROTHESAY,

1978–1979

DUNOON, ST.ANDREWS, MONTROSE, FALKIRK, PENICUIK, MUSSELBURGH, LIVINGSTON, TROON & ABOYNE

OPEN HOUSE
In-house Choreographic Workshops
PERFORMED IN GLASGOW

WINTER
Swan Lake
Choreographer: Marius Petipa / Lev Ivanov
Composer: Tchaikovsky
The Nutcracker
Choreographer: Peter Darrell / Lev Ivanov
Composer: Tchaikovsky
PERFORMED IN GLASGOW

1979
NEW WORK '79
Symphony in C
Choreographer: William Bowen
Composer: Stravinsky
Rendezvous
Choreographer: Susan Cooper
Composer: Claude Debussy
Dichotomy Singular
Choreographer: Roy Campbell-Moore
Composer: Karel Husa
Love Story 2002
Choreographer: Peter Royston
Composer: Darius Milhaud
Pastimes Passing
Choreographer: Anne Sholem
Composer: Leos Janácek
Snowflakes are Dancing
Choreographer: Michael Harper
Composer: Claude Debussy
Herzgewachse
Choreographer: Erica Knighton
Composer: Schoenberg
Aria
Choreographer: Garry Trinder
Composer: Stravinsky
Pteradacta
Choreographer: William Bowen
Composer: Steve Miller Band
PERFORMED IN GLASGOW

10TH ANNIVERSARY SPRING SEASON
Giselle
Choreographer: Peter Darrell / Jean Corelli / Jules Perrot
Composer: Adolphe Adam
Napoli
Choreographer: August Bournonville
Composer: Gade / Helsted / Pauli / Lumbye
Underground Rumours: Ursprung / The Water's Edge / Such Sweet Thunder
Choreographer: Royston Maldoom
Composer: Anderson
Tales of Hoffmann
Choreographer: Peter Darrell
Composer: Jacques Offenbach / Arr. Lanchberry
PERFORMED IN GLASGOW, EDINBURGH, LIVERPOOL, COVENTRY, HULL, ABERDEEN, INVERNESS, DARLINGTON, PERTH & BOURNEMOUTH

Swan Lake
Choreographer: Peter Darrell / Lev Ivanov

1979–1981

Composer: Tchaikovsky
PERFORMED IN EDINBURGH

SUMMER
Underground Rumours: Ursprung
Choreographer: Royston Maldoom
Composer: Jon Anderson
Napoli
Choreographer: August Bournonville
Composer: Gade / Helsted / Pauli / Lumbye
PERFORMED IN EDINBURGH & LONDON

AUTUMN
La Sylphide
Choreographer: August Bournonville
Composer: Hermann Lovenskjold
Vespri
Choreographer: André Prokovsky
Composer: Verdi
PERFORMED IN EDINBURGH

1980
GALA EVENING: GOLD-DIGGERS OF 1980
Cinderella (pas de deux)
Choreographer: Peter Darrell
Composer: Gioachino Rossini / Arr. Tovey
Blue Meadow
Corsaire (pas de deux)
Choreographer: Marius Petipa
Composer: Riccardo Drigo
Aftermath
In the Mist
Choreographer: Gordon Aitken
Composer: Leos Janácek
Five Rückert Songs
Choreographer: Peter Darrell
Composer: Gustav Mahler
Vespri
Choreographer: André Prokovsky
Composer: Verdi
PERFORMED IN GLASGOW

EDINBURGH INTERNATIONAL FESTIVAL
Chéri
Choreographer: Peter Darrell
Composer: David Earl
PERFORMED IN GLASGOW

AUTUMN
Giselle
Choreographer: Peter Darrell / Jean Corelli / Jules Perrot
Composer: Adolphe Adam
PERFORMED IN PERTH, DUNDEE & YORK

1981
SUMMER
Napoli
Choreographer: August Bournonville
Composer: Gade / Helsted / Pauli / Lumbye
Three Dances to Japanese Music
Choreographer: Jack Carter
Composer: Traditional Japanese
La Sylphide
Choreographer: August Bournonville
Composer: Hermann Lovenskjold
Napoli Act III
Choreographer: August Bournonville
Composer: Gade / Helsted / Pauli / Lumbye
Salome
Choreographer: Peter Darrell
Composer: Paul Hindemith

1981–1982

Five Rückert Songs
Choreographer: Peter Darrell
Composer: Gustav Mahler
Adagietto
Composer: Gustav Mahler
PERFORMED IN VENICE (ITALY) & SANTANDER (SPAIN)

SPANISH TOUR
Symphony in D
Choreographer: Jirí Kylián
Composer: Joseph Haydn
Three Dances to Japanese Music
Choreographer: Jack Carter
Composer: Traditional Japanese
La Sylphide
Choreographer: August Bournonville
Composer: Hermann Lovenskjold
PERFORMED IN SANTANDER, SAN SEBASTIAN & BIARRITZ (SPAIN)

AUTUMN
Symphony in D
Choreographer: Jirí Kylián
Composer: Joseph Haydn
Kp Index
Choreographer: Jack Carter
Composer: Electronic
Five Rückert Songs
Choreographer: Peter Darrell
Composer: Gustav Mahler
Ursprung
Choreographer: Royston Maldoom
Composer: Anderson
PERFORMED IN STIRLING & GLASGOW

WINTER 1981/1982
Cinderella
Choreographer: Peter Darrell
Composer: Gioachino Rossini / Arr. Tovey
PERFORMED IN GLASGOW & EDINBURGH

1982
THE NUTCRACKER
The Nutcracker
Choreographer: Peter Darrell / Lev Ivanov
Composer: Tchaikovsky
PERFORMED IN EDINBURGH

SPRING
Tales of Hoffmann
Choreographer: Peter Darrell
Composer: Jacques Offenbach / Arr. Lanchberry
PERFORMED IN EDINBURGH, INVERNESS & BRISTOL
Romeo & Juliet
Choreographer: John Cranko
Composer: Sergei Prokofiev
PERFORMED IN GLASGOW, EDINBURGH, INVERNESS, BRISTOL, BELFAST & PERTH
Napoli
Choreographer: August Bournonville
Composer: Gade / Helsted / Pauli / Lumbye
O Caritas
Choreographer: Peter Darrell
Composer: Toumazi / Taylor / Stevens
Five Rückert Songs
Choreographer: Peter Darrell
Composer: Gustav Mahler
Roccoco Variations
Choreographer: Peter Darrell
Composer: Tchaikovsky
PERFORMED IN BARCELONA (SPAIN)

1982

SUMMER
Vespri
Choreographer: André Prokovsky
Composer: Verdi
Othello
Choreographer: Peter Darrell
Composer: Franz Liszt
Ursprung
Choreographer: Peter Royston
Composer: Anderson

AUTUMN
Vespri
Choreographer: André Prokovsky
Composer: Verdi
Belong
Choreographer: Norbert Vesak
Composer: Syrinx
Five Rückert Songs
Choreographer: Peter Darrell
Composer: Gustav Mahler
Valse Excentrique
Choreographer: Kenneth MacMillan
Composer: Jacques Ibert
Pas de Quatre
Choreographer: Anton Dolin
Composer: Cesare Pugni
O Caritas
Choreographer: Peter Darrell
Composer: Toumazi / Taylor / Stevens
PERFORMED IN DONCASTER, DARLINGTON, SNAPE & TREORCHY

Symphony in D
Choreographer: Jirí Kylián
Composer: Joseph Haydn
Spectre de la Rose
Choreographer: Mikhail Fokine
Composer: Carl-Maria von Weber
Chéri
Choreographer: Peter Darrell
Composer: David Earl
PERFORMED IN GLASGOW & EDINBURGH

VARIETY PERFORMANCE
Valse Excentrique
Choreographer: Kenneth MacMillan
Composer: Jacques Ibert
Vespri
Choreographer: André Prokovsky
Composer: Verdi
PERFORMED IN ABERDEEN

STEPS SOUTH TOUR
Vespri
Choreographer: André Prokovsky
Composer: Verdi
Belong
Choreographer: Norbert Vesak
Composer: Syrinx
Five Rückert Songs
Choreographer: Peter Darrell
Composer: Gustav Mahler
Valse Excentrique
Choreographer: Kenneth MacMillan
Composer: Jacques Ibert
Pas de Quatre
Choreographer: Anton Dolin
Composer: Cesare Pugni
O Caritas
Choreographer: Peter Darrell
Composer: Toumazi / Taylor / Stevens
PERFORMED IN DONCASTER

1982–1983

ROMEO & JULIET
Romeo & Juliet
Choreographer: John Cranko
Composer: Sergei Prokofiev

CINDERELLA
Cinderella
(STV Recording – 30/12/82)
Choreographer: Peter Darrell
Composer: Gioachino Rossini /
Arr. Tovey
PERFORMED IN GLASGOW & EDINBURGH

1983
SWAN LAKE
Swan Lake
Choreographer: Peter Darrell /
Lev Ivanov
Composer: Tchaikovsky
PERFORMED IN GLASGOW, EDINBURGH,
ABERDEEN & INVERNESS

SPRING
Gardens of the Night
Choreographer: Peter Darrell
Composer: Frédéric Chopin
Quarrels Not Their Own
Choreographer: Peter Royston
Les Sylphides
Choreographer: Mikhail Fokine
Composer: Frédéric Chopin
PERFORMED IN GLASGOW,
EDINBURGH & INVERNESS

GISELLE
Giselle
Choreographer: Peter Darrell /
Jean Corelli / Jules Perrot
Composer: Adolphe Adam
PERFORMED IN LISBON (PORTUGAL),
BELFAST & GLASGOW

SUMMER
Three Dances to Japanese Music
Choreographer: Jack Carter
Composer: Traditional Japanese
Othello
Choreographer: Peter Darrell
Composer: Franz Liszt
Vespri
Choreographer: André Prokovsky
Composer: Verdi
PERFORMED IN GLASGOW
Three Dances to Japanese Music
Choreographer: Jack Carter
Composer: Traditional Japanese
Belong
Choreographer: Norbert Vesak
Composer: Syrinx
Five Rückert Songs
Choreographer: Peter Darrell
Composer: Gustav Mahler
Ursprung
Choreographer: Royston Maldoom
Composer: Anderson
PERFORMED IN ISTANBUL (TURKEY);
LIMASOLL, NICOSIA, PAPHOS (CYPRUS);
GRANADA (SPAIN)

AUTUMN
Symphony in D
Choreographer: Jiří Kylián
Composer: Joseph Haydn
La Sylphide
Choreographer: August Bournonville
Composer: Hermann Lovenskjold
PERFORMED IN GLASGOW & EDINBURGH

1983–1984

AUTUMN TRIPLE BILL:
La Ventana
Choreographer: August Bournonville
Composer: Hans Christian Lumbye
Prisoners
Choreographer: Peter Darrell
Composer: Béla Bartók
Paquita
Choreographer: Marius Petipa
Composer: Minkus
PERFORMED IN GLASGOW & EDINBURGH

AUTUMN MIXED BILL
La Ventana
Choreographer: August Bournonville
Composer: Hans Christian Lumbye
Flower Festival at Genzano
(pas de deux)
Choreographer: August Bournonville
Composer: Helsted / Paulli
Five Rückert Songs
Choreographer: Peter Darrell
Composer: Gustav Mahler
Randombach
Choreographer: Peter Royston
Composer: Bach
PERFORMED IN PITLOCHRY,
DUNFERMLINE, AYR & ABERDEEN

Full Call
Choreographer: Peter Royston
Randombach
Choreographer: Peter Royston
Composer: Bach
Shoals of Herring
Choreographer: Royston Maldoom
Composer: Traditional Scots /
Magdalen Green
Three Dances to Japanese Music
Choreographer: Jack Carter
Composer: Traditional Japanese
PERFORMED IN PAISLEY, ERSKINE,
BELLSHILL, MILTON, GLASGOW,
CUMBERNAULD, PITLOCHRY,
AYR & ABERDEEN
Belong
Choreographer: Norbert Vesak
Composer: Syrinx
Five Rückert Songs
Choreographer: Peter Darrell
Composer: Gustav Mahler
Vespri
Choreographer: André Prokovsky
Composer: Verdi
PERFORMED IN PRESTON, BATH,
BARNSLEY, BILLINGHAM, BUXTON;
AMMAN (JORDAN) & ATHENS (GREECE)

1984
THE NUTCRACKER
The Nutcracker
Choreographer: Peter Darrell /
Lev Ivanov
Composer: Tchaikovsky
PERFORMED IN GLASGOW & ABERDEEN

ROMEO & JULIET
Romeo & Juliet
Choreographer: John Cranko
Composer: Sergei Prokofiev
PERFORMED IN GLASGOW,
EDINBURGH & ABERDEEN

TALES OF HOFFMANN
Tales of Hoffmann
Choreographer: Peter Darrell
Composer: Jacques Offenbach /
Arr. Lanchberry

1984–1985

PERFORMED IN INVERNESS,
GLASGOW & BELFAST

SUMMER
Offenbach Suite
Choreographer: Various
Composer: Jacques Offenbach
O Caritas
Choreographer: Peter Darrell
Composer: Toumazi /
Taylor / Stevens
Sylvia (pas de deux)
Choreographer: Gordon Aitken
Composer: Leo Delibes
Shoals of Herring
Choreographer: Royston Maldoom
Composer: Traditional Scots /
Magdalen Green
PERFORMED IN WICK, BRORA,
DINGWALL, LOCHABER, ROTHESAY,
OBAN, PORTREE & THURSO

1985
THE NUTCRACKER
The Nutcracker
Choreographer: Peter Darrell /
Lev Ivanov
Composer: Tchaikovsky
PERFORMED IN ABERDEEN & BELFAST

BALLET FOR SCOTLAND TOUR
Three Dances to Japanese Music
Choreographer: Jack Carter
Composer: Traditional Japanese
Water's Edge
Choreographer: Robert North
Composer: Jethro Tull
Sylvia (pas de deux)
Choreographer: Gordon Aitken
Composer: Leo Delibes
Shoals of Herring
Choreographer: Royston Maldoom
Composer: Traditional Scots /
Magdalen Green
PERFORMED IN GLASGOW, EDINBURGH,
DUNFERMLINE & ST. ANDREWS

SPRING
Hail the Classical!
Choreographer: Michael Clark
Composer: The Fall
Remembered Dances
Choreographer: Christopher Bruce
Composer: Leos Janácek
Pococurantis
Choreographer: Peter Royston
Composer: Thomas Robinson
Gut Reactions
PERFORMED IN GLASGOW & ABERDEEN

SWAN LAKE
Swan Lake
Choreographer: Peter Darrell /
Lev Ivanov
Composer: Tchaikovsky
PERFORMED IN BRISTOL,
LIVERPOOL, EDINBURGH, GLASGOW,
INVERNESS & BELFAST

SUMMER
La Sylphide
Choreographer: August Bournonville
Composer: Hermann Lovenskjold
Symphony in D
Choreographer: Jiří Kylián
Composer: Joseph Haydn
PERFORMED IN EDINBURGH

1985–1986

CARMEN
Carmen
Choreographer: Peter Darrell
Composer: Bizet / Arr. Muldowney
PERFORMED IN EDINBURGH,
ABERDEEN, GLASGOW, LIVERPOOL,
NEWCASTLE & BELFAST

BALLET FOR SCOTLAND TOUR
Napoli Act II
Choreographer: August Bournonville
Composer: Gade / Helsted /
Pauli / Lumbye
Peasant pas de deux (Giselle)
Choreographer: Peter Darrell
Composer: Adolphe Adam
Othello
Choreographer: Peter Darrell
Composer: Franz Liszt
PERFORMED IN DUNDEE,
CUMBERNAULD, WISHAW,
INVERURIE, FALKIRK, KILMARNOCK,
DUMFRIES, PLOCKTON, CROOKSTON,
LINLITHGOW, WICK, ACHARACLE,
INVERNESS & ABERDEEN

AUTUMN
Napoli Act II
Choreographer: August Bournonville
Composer: Gade / Helsted /
Pauli / Lumbye
Remembered Dances
Choreographer: Christopher Bruce
Composer: Leos Janácek
Giselle
Choreographer: Peter Darrell /
Jean Corelli / Jules Perrot
Composer: Adolphe Adam
Othello
Choreographer: Peter Darrell
Composer: Franz Liszt

CHRISTMAS 1985
The Nutcracker
Choreographer: Peter Darrell /
Lev Ivanov
Composer: Tchaikovsky
PERFORMED IN EDINBURGH,
GLASGOW, ABERDEEN & HULL

1986
HONG KONG TOUR
Symphony in D
Choreographer: Jiří Kylián
Composer: Joseph Haydn
La Sylphide
Choreographer: August Bournonville
Composer: Hermann Lovenskjold
Napoli Act II
Choreographer: August Bournonville
Composer: Gade / Helsted /
Pauli / Lumbye
Black Swan (pas de deux)
Choreographer: Peter Darrell
Composer: Tchaikovsky
Remembered Dances
Choreographer: Christopher Bruce
Composer: Leos Janácek
Othello
Choreographer: Peter Darrell
Composer: Franz Liszt

AUSTRALIAN TOUR
Carmen
Choreographer: Peter Darrell
Composer: Bizet / Arr. Muldowney
PERFORMED IN PERTH (AUSTRALIA)

1986

SPRING
Napoli Act II
Choreographer: August Bournonville
Composer: Gade / Helsted /
Pauli / Lumbye
PERFORMED IN GLASGOW,
ABERDEEN & EDINBURGH

TRIPLE BILL
Symphony in D
Choreographer: Jiří Kylián
Composer: Joseph Haydn
La Spectre de la Rose
Choreographer: Mikhail Fokine
Composer: Carl-Maria von Weber
Chéri
Choreographer: Peter Darrell
Composer: David Earl
PERFORMED IN BELFAST & GLASGOW

DOUBLE BILL
Three Dances to Japanese Music
Choreographer: Jack Carter
Composer: Traditional Japanese
La Sylphide
Choreographer: August Bournonville
Composer: Hermann Lovenskjold
PERFORMED IN CHARLESTON (USA)

SUMMER
Symphony in D
Choreographer: Jiří Kylián
Composer: Joseph Haydn
Remembered Dances
Choreographer: Christopher Bruce
Composer: Leos Janácek
Cinderella pas de deux
Choreographer: Peter Darrell
Composer: Gioachino Rossini /
Arr. Tovey
Othello
Choreographer: Peter Darrell
Composer: Franz Liszt
PERFORMED IN CHARLESTON (USA)

MIXED BILL:
Vespri
Choreographer: André Prokovsky
Composer: Verdi
Le Corsaire
Choreographer: Marius Petipa
Composer: Riccardo Drigo
Remembered Dances
Choreographer: Christopher Bruce
Composer: Leos Janácek
Irmelin
Choreographer: Peter Darrell
Composer: Delius
PERFORMED IN CHARLESTON (USA)

TOUR OF ITALY
Ursprung
Choreographer: Royston Maldoom
Composer: Anderson
Giselle
Choreographer: Peter Darrell /
Jean Corelli / Jules Perrot
Composer: Adolphe Adam
The Nutcracker (excerpts)
Choreographer: Peter Darrell /
Lev Ivanov
Composer: Tchaikovsky
Valse Excentrique
Choreographer: Kenneth MacMillan
Composer: Jacques Ibert
PERFORMED IN SPOLETO, PERGINE,
REGGIO EMILIA, LUGO (ITALY)
& PALERMO (SICILY)

1986–1987

BALLET FOR SCOTLAND TOUR
O Caritas
Choreographer: Peter Darrell
Composer: Toumazi / Taylor / Stevens
Catulli Carmina
Choreographer: Paulo Lopes
Composer: Carl Orff
The Nutcracker (excerpts)
Choreographer: Peter Darrell / Lev Ivanov
Composer: Tchaikovsky
O Caritas
Choreographer: Peter Darrell
Composer: Toumazi / Taylor / Stevens
PERFORMED IN DENNY, BELLSHILL, LARGS, CLYDEBANK, GARTHAMLOCK, FALKIRK, EDINBURGH, LINLITHGOW, STRANRAER, KILMARNOCK, EDINBURGH, DUNFERMLINE, OBAN & ELGIN

AUTUMN
Giselle
Choreographer: Peter Darrell / Jean Corelli / Jules Perrot
Composer: Adolphe Adam
PERFORMED IN BATH, LIVERPOOL, ABERDEEN, INVERNESS, EDINBURGH & GLASGOW

1987
WINTER TOUR
Cinderella
Choreographer: Peter Darrell
Composer: Gioachino Rossini / arr. Tovey
The Nutcracker
Choreographer: Peter Darrell / Lev Ivanov
Composer: Tchaikovsky
Five Rückert Songs
Choreographer: Peter Darrell
Composer: Gustav Mahler
PERFORMED IN GLASGOW, ABERDEEN, HULL, EDINBURGH & BELFAST

BALLET FOR SCOTLAND TOUR
Othello
Choreographer: Peter Darrell
Composer: Franz Liszt
PERFORMED IN ST. ANDREWS, PORTABELLO, ALLOA & CRIEFF

BALLET FOR IRELAND TOUR
Catulli Carmina
Choreographer: Paulo Lopez
Composer: Carl Orff
Napoli Act II
Choreographer: August Bournonville
Composer: Gade / Helsted / Pauli / Lumbye
Five Rückert Songs
Choreographer: Peter Darrell
Composer: Gustav Mahler
PERFORMED IN ENNISKILLEN, LARNE, COLERAINE, LONDONDERRY, NEWRY, DOWNPATRICK, NEWTONARDS & BALLYMENA

SPRING TOUR
Tales of Hoffmann
Choreographer: Peter Darrell
Composer: Jacques Offenbach
Three Dances to Japanese Music
Choreographer: Jack Carter
Composer: Traditional Japanese

1987–1988

Economy in a Straight Jacket
Choreographer: Peter Darrell
Composer: Bach
Picnic
Choreographer: Peter Darrell
Composer: Poulenc
PERFORMED IN GLASGOW, EDINBURGH, ABERDEEN, NEWCASTLE, WICK, BRORA & TAIN

BALLET FOR SCOTLAND TOUR
Les Sylphides
Choreographer: Mikhail Fokine
Composer: Frédéric Chopin
Vespri
Choreographer: André Prokovsky
Composer: Verdi
Prisoners
Peter Darrell
Composer: Béla Bartók
PERFORMED IN DINGWALL, FORT WILLIAM, INVERURIE, ABOYNE, ELGIN, PORTOBELLO, DUNFERMLINE & DUMBARTON

WINTER
Skazka
Choreographer: Various
Composer: Various / Arr. Hamilton

Death of Peter Darrell, 2 December

1988
THE NUTCRACKER
The Nutcracker
Choreographer: Peter Darrell / Lev Ivanov
Composer: Tchaikovsky
PERFORMED IN GLASGOW, ABERDEEN, NEWCASTLE, EDINBURGH, BELFAST & HULL

TRIBUTE TO PETER DARRELL
Five Rückert Songs
Choreographer: Peter Darrell
Composer: Gustav Mahler
Chéri
Choreographer: Peter Darrell
Composer: David Earl
PERFORMED IN GLASGOW

New Artistic Director: Elaine McDonald

SPRING/SUMMER
Romeo & Juliet
Choreographer: John Cranko
Composer: Sergei Prokofiev
PERFORMED IN ABERDEEN, EDINBURGH, INVERNESS, NEWCASTLE, HULL & GLASGOW

AUTUMN
Three Dances to Japanese Music
Choreographer: Jack Carter
Composer: Traditional Japanese
Sonata in Time
Choreographer: Michael Corder
Composer: Stravinsky / Schubert / Scarlatti
Cheri
Choreographer: Peter Darrell
Composer: David Earl

GISELLE
Giselle
Choreographer: Peter Darrell / Jean Corelli / Jules Perrot
Composer: Adolphe Adam
PERFORMED IN CANTERBURY, NOTTINGHAM & DARLINGTON

1988–1989

NATIONAL TOUR
Hommage to Nordi
Choreographer: Elaine McDonald
Composer: Verdi
Don Quixote
Choreographer: Marius Petipa
Composer: Minkus
Prix de Rome
Choreographer: Lloyd Embleton
Composer: Maurice Ravel
Swan Lake
Choreographer: Peter Darrell / Lev Ivanov
Composer: Tchaikovsky
Shoals of Herring
Choreographer: Royston Maldoom
Composer: Traditional Scots / Magdalen Green
PERFORMED IN GLASGOW

NATIONAL TOUR
Vespri
Choreographer: André Prokovsky
Composer: Verdi
Sleeping Beauty (pas de deux)
Choreographer: Marius Petipa
Composer: Tchaikovsky
Prisoners
Choreographer: Peter Darrell
Composer: Béla Bartók
Prix de Rome
Choreographer: Lloyd Embleton
Composer: Maurice Ravel
PERFORMED IN BUILTH, WELLS, BRECON, ABERYSTWYTH, HARLECH, NEWTOWN, DOWNPATRICK, NEWTONARDS, COLERAINE, LARNE, ENNISKILLEN, LONDONDERRY & NEWRY

NATIONAL TOUR
Hommage to Nordi
Choreographer: Elaine McDonald
Composer: Verdi
Pas de Deux Don Quixote
Choreographer: Marius Petipa
Composer: Minkus
Shoals of Herring
Choreographer: Royston Maldoom
Composer: Traditional Scots / Magdalen Green
Sonata In Time
Choreographer: Michael Corder
Composer: Scarlatti / Stravinsky / Schubert
PERFORMED IN CUMBERNAULD, BRORA, WICK, NAIRN, ELGIN, ABOYNE, INVERURIE, PORTOBELLO, ALLOA, FALKIRK, FORT WILLIAM, DINGWALL, STRANRAER, KILMARNOCK, DUNFERMLINE & DUMFRIES

New Artistic Director: Nanette Glushak

1989
PETER PAN
Peter Pan
Choreographer: Graham Lustig
Composer: Edward McGuire
PERFORMED IN GLASGOW, OXFORD, HULL, INVERNESS, BELFAST, EDINBURGH, BRISTOL & ABERDEEN

SUMMER
Pas de Fiancées
Choreographer: Jack Carter
Composer: Tchaikovsky

1989–1990

Belong
Choreographer: Norbert Vesak
Composer: Syrinx
Cinderella (pas de deux)
Choreographer: Peter Darrell
Composer: Gioachino Rossini / Arr. Tovey
The Nutcracker (pas de deux)
Choreographer: Peter Darrell / Lev Ivanov
Composer: Tchaikovsky
Prisoners
Choreographer: Peter Darrell
Composer: Béla Bartók
PERFORMED IN GLASGOW, TAIN, WICK, BRORA, NAIRN & BRAEMAR

AUTUMN
Symphony in D
Choreographer: Jirí Kylián
Composer: Joseph Haydn
Pas de Fiancées
Choreographer: Jack Carter
Composer: Tchaikovsky
Chéri
Choreographer: Peter Darrell
Composer: David Earl
PERFORMED IN DARLINGTON & CANTERBURY

AUTUMN
Petrushka
Choreographer: Oleg Vinogradova
Composer: Igor Stravinsky
Kirov Diverts
Choreographer: Natalia Vinogradova
Composer: Drigo / Pugni / Minkus
Prisoners
Choreographer: Peter Darrell
Composer: Béla Bartók
Symphony in D
Choreographer: Jirí Kylián
Composer: Joseph Haydn
La Sylphide
Choreographer: August Bournonville
Composer: Hermann Lovenskjold
PERFORMED IN NEWCASTLE, GLASGOW & ABERDEEN

PETER PAN
Peter Pan
Choreographer: Graham Lustig
Composer: Edward McGuire
PERFORMED IN GLASGOW

1990
SPRING
Who Cares?
Choreographer: George Balanchine
Composer: Gershwin / Kay
Paquita
Choreographer: Oleg Vinogradova
Composer: Minkus
Scotch Symphony
Choreographer: George Balanchine
Composer: Mendelssohn
PERFORMED IN GLASGOW, HULL, NEWCASTLE & EDINBURGH

NATIONAL TOUR
Three Dances to Japanese Music
Choreographer: Jack Carter
Composer: Traditional Japanese
Fairy Doll
Choreographer: Nikolai & Sergei Legat
Composer: Cesare Pugni

1990–1991

Othello
Choreographer: Peter Darrell
Composer: Franz Liszt
La Esmeralda (pas de six)
Choreographer: Jules Perrot
Composer: Cesare Pugni
Paquita
Choreographer: Oleg Vinogradova
Composer: Drigo / Pugni / Minkus
Belong
Choreographer: Norbert Vesak
Composer: Syrinx
Zwei Gesange
Choreographer: Ennio Morricone
Composer: Brahms
Sun and Steel
Choreographer: Ennio Morricone
Composer: Guy Hamilton
Pretty Ugly
Choreographer: Amanda Miller
Composer: Scherer / Lindsay
Aquarelle
Choreographer: Michel Rahn
Composer: Bach / Stokowski
Raymonda (pas de deux)
Choreographer: Marius Petipa / Galina Samsova
Composer: Glazunov
Lilac Garden
Choreographer: Antony Tudor
Composer: Chausson
PERFORMED IN DUMFRIES, BUITH WELLS, ABERYSTWYTH, HEXHAM, DUNFERMLINE, KILMARNOCK, FELINFACH, DINGWALL, BRORA, WICK, DOWNPATRICK, COLERAINE, NAIRN, BRECON, LARNE, ARMAGH, ENNISKILLEN, DONAGHMORE, GLASGOW, EDINBURGH & ABERDEEN

New Artistic Director: Galina Samsova

JAPANESE TOUR
Forgotten Land
Choreographer: Jirí Kylián
Composer: Britten
Petrushka
Choreographer: Oleg Vinogradova
Composer: Igor Stravinsky
Chéri
Choreographer: Peter Darrell
Composer: David Earl
PERFORMED IN KOBE (JAPAN)

ROMEO & JULIET
Romeo & Juliet
Choreographer: John Cranko
Composer: Sergei Prokofiev
PERFORMED IN HONG KONG (CHINA) & TOKYO (JAPAN)

WINTER TOUR
The Nutcracker
Choreographer: Peter Darrell / Lev Ivanov
Composer: Tchaikovsky
PERFORMED IN GLASGOW, DUBLIN & ABERDEEN.

1991
SCOTTISH BALLET 2 ROYAL PERFORMANCE IN THE PRESENCE OF HM THE QUEEN
Esprit
Choreographer: Paolo Lopes
Composer: Edward McGuire
PERFORMED IN PRESTWICK

1991

Swan Lake Tour
Swan Lake
Choreographer:
Peter Darrell / Lev Ivanov
Composer: Tchaikovsky
Performed in Glasgow, Belfast, Hull, Liverpool, Aberdeen, Edinburgh & Sheffield

Spring
Three Dances to Japanese Music
Choreographer: Jack Carter
Composer: Traditional Japanese
Napoli Act III
Choreographer:
August Bournonville
Composer: Gade / Helsted / Pauli / Lumbye
Les Sylphides
Choreographer: Mikhail Fokine
Composer: Frédéric Chopin
Performed in Sheffield

Choreographic Workshops
Cliffhanger
Choreographer: Maxine Railton
Two Nocturnes
Choreographer: Lloyd Embleton
All in a Daze Work
Choreographer: Rosemary O'Donnell
For Ours to See
Choreographer: Karl Burnett
Canzonetta
Choreographer: Michael Rolnick
Backward Glances
Choreographer: Jane Jewell
Toccata
Choreographer: Michael Rolnick
Performed in Glasgow

Spring/Summer Tour
Napoli Act III
Choreographer:
August Bournonville
Composer: Gade / Helsted / Pauli / Lumbye
Othello
Choreographer: Peter Darrell
Composer: Franz Liszt
Les Sylphides
Choreographer: Mikhail Fokine
Composer: Frédéric Chopin
Performed in Dundee, Stirling, Kirkcaldy & Glasgow

Royal Gala Performance
Napoli Act III
Choreographer:
August Bournonville
Composer: Gade / Helsted / Pauli / Lumbye
Othello
Choreographer: Peter Darrell
Composer: Franz Liszt
Five Dances in the Manner of Isadora Duncan
Choreographer:
Frederick Ashton
Composer: Brahms
Monotones
Choreographer:
Frederick Ashton
Composer: Erik Satie
Performed in Forfar

1991–1992

Giselle Tour
Giselle
(Peter Darrell Production)
Choreographer: Peter Darrell / Jean Corelli / Jules Perrot
Composer: Adolphe Adam
Performed in Glasgow, Aberdeen, Inverness, Liverpool, Edinburgh, Hull & Newcastle

Summer/Autumn Tour
Troy Game
Choreographer: Robert North
Composer: Batucada / Downes
Vespri
Choreographer: André Prokovsky
Composer: Verdi
Concerto Barocco
Choreographer: George Balanchine
Composer: Bach
Performed in Glasgow, Aberdeen, Inverness, Hull & Newcastle

Autumn
Forgotten Land
Choreographer: Jirí Kylián
Composer: Britten
Performed in London

Winter
Cinderella
Choreographer: Peter Darrell
Composer: Gioachino Rossini / Arr. Tovey
Performed in Glasgow & Aberdeen

1992

Coppélia Tour
Coppélia
Choreographer: Peter Wright / Marius Petipa
Composer: Leo Delibes
Performed in Glasgow, Aberdeen, Inverness, Edinburgh, Newcastle, Hull & Belfast

Spring Triple Bill
Troy Game
Choreographer: Robert North
Composer: Batucada / Downes
Sea of Troubles
Choreographer: Kenneth MacMillan
Composer: Martinu
Brief
Choreographer: Amanda Miller
Composer: Bach
Performed in Glasgow

Russian Tour
Troy Game
Choreographer: Robert North
Composer: Batucada / Downes
Vespri
Choreographer: André Prokovsky
Composer: Verdi
Forgotten Land
Choreographer: Jirí Kylián
Composer: Britten
Who Cares?
Choreographer: George Balanchine
Composer: Gershwin / Kay
Brief
Choreographer: Amanda Miller
Composer: Bach
Symphony in D
Choreographer: Jirí Kylián
Composer: Joseph Haydn
Performed in St. Petersburg, Moscow (Russia) & Kiev (Ukraine)

1992–1993

Romeo & Juliet Tour
Romeo & Juliet
Choreographer: John Cranko
Composer: Sergei Prokofiev
Performed in Glasgow, Aberdeen, Sheffield, Edinburgh & Hull

Summer Triple Bill
Who Cares?
Choreographer: George Balanchine
Composer: George Gershwin
Brief
Choreographer: Amanda Miller
Composer: Bach
Overgrown Path
Choreographer: Jirí Kylián
Composer: Leos Janácek
Performed in Glasgow, Sheffield & Hull

Japanese Tour
Coppélia
Choreographer: Peter Wright / Marius Petipa
Composer: Leo Delibes
The Nutcracker
Choreographer: Peter Darrell / Lev Ivanov
Composer: Tchaikovsky
Performed in Tokyo, Osaka (Japan), & Seoul (South Korea)

1993
Spring
A Midsummer Night's Dream
Choreographer: Robert Cohan
Composer: Mendelssohn / Pheloung
Performed in Glasgow, Edinburgh, Liverpool, Inverness, Aberdeen, Hull & Ottawa (Canada)

Summer
Overgrown Path
Choreographer: Jirí Kylián
Composer: Leos Janácek
Troy Game
Choreographer: Robert North
Composer: Batucada / Downes
Concerto Barocco
Choreographer: George Balanchine
Composer: Bach
Performed in Leicester & Glasgow

Autumn
Bruch Violin Concerto
Choreographer: Clark Tippett
Composer: Bruch
Othello
Choreographer: Peter Darrell
Composer: Franz Liszt
Anna Karenina
Choreographer: André Prokovsky
Composer: Tchaikovsky / arr. Wooldenden
Performed in Glasgow, Edinburgh, Aberdeen, Liverpool, Hull, Sheffield & Inverness

Winter Scottish Ballet 2 Tour
Performed in Dundee, Goole, Epwarth, Motherwell, Falkirk, Perth, Colchester, Dumfries, Wick, Brora, Islay, Musselburgh, Solihull, Haddo, Fort William, Kingussie, Elgin, Dingwall, Plockton, Stranraer, Glenrothes, Preston, Harlow & Oban

1993–1995

Peter Pan Tour
Peter Pan
Choreographer: Graham Lustig
Composer: Edward McGuire
Performed in Glasgow, Edinburgh & Aberdeen

1994
Spring
Sleeping Beauty
Choreographer: Marius Petipa / Galina Samsova
Composer: Tchaikovsky
Performed in Glasgow, Aberdeen, Oxford, Newcastle, Hull, Edinburgh & Inverness

Summer Shorts Tour
Raymonda pas de dix
Choreographer: Marius Petipa / Galina Samsova
Composer: Glazunov
Belong
Choreographer: Norbert Vesak
Composer: Syrinx
Overgrown Path
Choreographer: Jirí Kylián
Composer: Leos Janácek
Scotch Symphony
Choreographer: George Balanchine
Composer: Mendelssohn
Performed in Stirling & Kirkcaldy

Cinderella Tour
Cinderella
Choreographer: Peter Darrell
Composer: Gioachino Rossini / arr. Tovey
Performed in Glasgow, Edinburgh, Aberdeen, Hull & Newcastle

The Nutcracker Tour
The Nutcracker
Choreographer: Peter Darrell / Lev Ivanov
Composer: Tchaikovsky
Performed in Glasgow, Edinburgh, Aberdeen & Seville (Spain)

1995
Swan Lake Tour
Swan Lake
Choreographer: Marius Petipa / Lev Ivanov / Galina Samsova
Composer: Tchaikovsky
Performed in Glasgow, Edinburgh, Hull, Woking, Inverness, Aberdeen, Newcastle & Belfast

Spring into Summer Tour
Shoals of Herring
Choreographer: Royston Maldoom
Composer: Traditional Scots / Magdalen Green
L'Après-midi d'un Faune
Choreographer: Cristian Uboldi
Composer: Claude Debussy
Flower Festival at Genzano (pas de deux)
Choreographer: August Bournonville
Composer: Helsted / Paulli
Fairy Doll
Choreographer: Nikolai and Sergei Legat
Composer: Riccardo Drigo
Les Sylphides
Choreographer: Mikhail Fokine
Composer: Frédéric Chopin

1995–1996

Joseph Haydn Pieces
Choreographer: Mark Baldwin
Composer: Joseph Haydn
Chéri
Choreographer: Peter Darrell
Composer: David Earl
Performed in Fort William, Wick, Dornoch, Banchory, Inverurie, Fraserburgh, Aboyne & Montrose

Autumn Tour
Coppélia
Choreographer: Peter Wright
Composer: Leo Delibes
A Midsummer Night's Dream
Choreographer: Robert Cohan
Composer: Mendelssohn / Pheloung
Performed in Aberdeen, Glasgow, Edinburgh, Newcastle & Hull

Peter Pan Tour
Peter Pan
Choreographer: Graham Lustig
Composer: Edward McGuire
Performed in Inverness, Edinburgh & Glasgow

1996
Spring
Ae Fond Kiss
Choreographer: Mark Baldwin
Composer: Igor Stravinsky
La Sylphide
Choreographer: August Bournonville
Composer: Hermann Lovenskjold
Performed in Glasgow, Edinburgh, Aberdeen, Inverness, Newcastle & Hull

National Tour
That Certain Feeling
Choreographer: André Prokovsky
Composer: George Gershwin
Belong (pas de deux)
Choreographer: Norbert Vesak
Composer: Syrinx
La Esmeralda (pas de deux)
Choreographer: Jules Perrot
Composer: Cesare Pugni
Shoals of Herring (pas de deux)
Choreographer: Royston Maldoom
Composer: Traditional Scots / Magdalen Green
More Poulenc
Choreographer: Mark Baldwin
Composer: Poulenc
Performed in Cumbernauld, Montrose, Inverurie, Irvine, Stranraer, Inverness, Peterhead, Dumbarton, Alloa, Ayr, Dundee, Haddo, Fort William, Wick, Dornoch, Elgin & Dunfermline

Sweat Baroque & Roll Tour
Joseph Haydn Pieces
Choreographer: Mark Baldwin
Composer: Joseph Haydn
Four Seasons
Choreographer: Robert Cohan
Composer: Vivaldi
Troy Game
Choreographer: Robert North
Composer: Batucada / Downes
Performed in Glasgow, Edinburgh, Norwich, Stirling & Aberdeen

1996–1998

WINTER 1996/1997
THE NUTCRACKER TOUR
The Nutcracker
Choreographer: Peter Darrell
Composer: Tchaikovsky
PERFORMED IN HULL, ABERDEEN, GLASGOW, EDINBURGH & BLACKPOOL

1997
SPRING
Troy Game
Choreographer: Robert North
Composer: Batucada / Downes
La Sylphide
Choreographer: August Bournonville
Composer: Hermann Lovenskjold
PERFORMED IN WOKING HIGH, WYCOMBE & SHEFFIELD

ROMEO & JULIET TOUR
Romeo & Juliet
Choreographer: John Cranko
Composer: Sergei Prokofiev
PERFORMED IN GLASGOW, EDINBURGH, ABERDEEN, NEWCASTLE & HULL

NATIONAL TOUR
Classical Divertissements
Vespri
Choreographer: André Prokovsky
Composer: Verdi
Tam O'Shanter
Choreographer: Lorna Scott
Composer: Malcolm Arnold
PERFORMED IN FORT WILLIAM, HADDO HOUSE, ELGIN, WICK, BRORA, PERTH, STIRLING, DUNDEE, KIRKCALDY, MOTHERWELL, ACHARACLE, PORTREE, PLOCKTON, STORNOWAY, ABOYNE, INVERURIE & OBAN

Artistic Director (acting): Kenn Burke

NATIONAL TOUR
Shoals of Herring
Choreographer: Royston Maldoom
Composer: Traditional Scots / Magdalen Green
Les Sylphides
Choreographer: Mikhail Fokine
Composer: Frédéric Chopin
PERFORMED IN DOWNPATRICK, BENBECULA, CASTLEBAY, ENNISKILLEN, DERRY, COLERAINE & LARNE

WINTER TOUR 1997/1998
La Fille Mal Gardée
Choreographer: Frederick Ashton
Composer: Ferdinand Hérold / Arr. Lanchberry
PERFORMED IN GLASGOW, ABERDEEN & EDINBURGH

1998
TALES OF HOFFMANN TOUR
Tales of Hoffmann
Choreographer: Peter Darrell
Composer: Jacques Offenbach / Arr. Lanchberry
PERFORMED IN GLASGOW, NEWCASTLE & EDINBURGH

COOL CLASSICS TOUR
Mosaic
Choreographer: Lorna Scott / Jane Jewell / Catarina Lappin
Composer: Various 20th-century composers

1997–1999

Bitter Destiny
Choreographer: Ivan Dinev
Composer: Tchaikovsky
First Movement
Choreographer: Micaela Greganti
Composer: Sergei Prokofiev
PERFORMED IN MUSSELBURGH, IRVINE, INVERNESS, PITLOCHRY, STIRLING, MOTHERWELL, GLASGOW, EDINBURGH, FALKIRK & GREENOCK

AUTUMN
Just Scratchin' the Surface
Choreographer: Adam Cooper
Composer: Ellington / Peterson / Mingus / Adler
Five Rückert Songs
Choreographer: Peter Darrell
Composer: Gustav Mahler
Faerie Feet
Choreographer: Sheridan Nicol
Composer: Peat Bog Faeries
PERFORMED IN GLASGOW

WINTER 1998/1989
CINDERELLA
Cinderella
Choreographer: Peter Darrell
Composer: Gioachino Rossini / Arr. Tovey
PERFORMED IN EDINBURGH, GLASGOW & ABERDEEN

LA FILLE MAL GARDÉE
La Fille Mal Gardée
Choreographer: Frederick Ashton
Composer: Ferdinand Hérold / Arr. Lanchberry
PERFORMED IN EDINBURGH, GLASGOW, INVERNESS, NOTTINGHAM & HULL

1999
SPRING
La Sylphide
Choreographer: August Bournonville
Composer: Hermann Lovenskjold
Light Fandango
Choreographer: Robert North
Composer: Appalachia Waltz / Old Blind Dogs
Triple: Rapture
Choreographer: Lila York
Composer: Sergei Prokofiev
Night Life
Choreographer: Tim Rushton
Composer: Bach
Diversions
Choreographer: Kenneth MacMillan
Composer: Sir Arthur Bliss
PERFORMED IN GLASGOW, ABERDEEN, EDINBURGH, PERTH, SADLER'S WELLS & LONDON

Artistic Director: Robert North

30TH ANNIVERSARY SEASON
Tales of Hoffmann
Choreographer: Peter Darrell
Composer: Jacques Offenbach / Arr. Lanchberry
PERFORMED IN INVERNESS & ABERDEEN
Giselle
Choreographer: Marius Petipa
Composer: Adolphe Adam
PERFORMED IN SPAIN, FRANCE, GLASGOW & INVERNESS

2000–2001

2000
WINTER
Offenbach & The Underworld
Choreographer: Robert North
Composer: Offenbach / Stravinsky
Prince Rama and the Demons
Choreographer: Robert North
Composer: Christopher Benstead
PERFORMED IN GLASGOW, WOKING, EDINBURGH, INVERNESS & ABERDEEN

SUMMER
Prince Rama and the Demons
Choreographer: Robert North
Composer: Christopher Benstead
PERFORMED IN FORT WILLIAM, OBAN, BERWICK-UPON-TWEED, MUSSELBURGH, AYR, ELGIN, WICK, IRVINE, ULLAPOOL, ABOYNE, ABERDEENSHIRE & DUNOON

SUMMER SEASON TRIPLE BILL
Miniatures
Choreographer: Robert North
Composer: Igor Stravinsky
Frédéric
Choreographer: Mehmet Balkan
Composer: Frédéric Chopin
Light Fandango
Choreographer: Robert North
Composer: Ma / Meyer / O'Connor / Traditional Irish
PERFORMED IN DUNFERMLINE, MONTROSE & GALASHIELS

ROMEO & JULIET
Romeo & Juliet
Choreographer: Robert North
Composer: Sergei Prokofiev
PERFORMED IN GLASGOW

SUMMER SEASON TRIPLE BILL
Miniatures
Choreographer: Robert North
Composer: Igor Stravinsky
Frédéric
Choreographer: Mehmet Balkan
Composer: Frédéric Chopin
Light Fandango
Choreographer: Robert North
Composer: Ma / Meyer / O'Connor / Traditional Irish
PERFORMED IN ROSS-ON-WYE

ROMEO & JULIET TOUR
Romeo & Juliet
Choreographer: Robert North
Composer: Sergei Prokofiev
PERFORMED IN ABERDEEN, EDINBURGH & INVERNESS

WINTER 2000/2001
Aladdin
Choreographer: Robert Cohan
Composer: Carl Davis
PERFORMED IN EDINBURGH, INVERNESS, ABERDEEN, HULL & GLASGOW

2001
ROMEO & JULIET TOUR
Romeo & Juliet
Choreographer: Robert North
Composer: Sergei Prokofiev
PERFORMED IN BELFAST

SPRING
Carmen
Choreographer: Robert North
Composer: Christopher Benstead
PERFORMED IN EDINBURGH, INVERNESS, ABERDEEN & GLASGOW

2001–2003

AUTUMN
In and Out
Choreographer: Hans van Manen
Composer: Anderson / Hagen
Sarcasms
Choreographer: Hans van Manen
Composer: Sergei Prokofiev
Death and the Maiden
Choreographer: Robert North
Composer: Schubert
Troy Game
Choreographer: Robert North
Composer: Batucada / Downes
PERFORMED IN GLASGOW, ABERDEEN & EDINBURGH

WINTER SEASON 2001/2002
THE SNOWMAN
The Snowman
Choreographer: Robert North
Composer: Howard Blake
PERFORMED IN GLASGOW, EDINBURGH, ABERDEEN & INVERNESS

2002
SPRING
Bach Dances and The Two Pigeons
Choreographer: Robert North / Frederick Ashton
Composer: Bach / Andre Messager
PERFORMED IN EDINBURGH, ABERDEEN, GLASGOW & INVERNESS

CARMEN
Carmen
Choreographer: Robert North
Composer: Christopher Benstead
PERFORMED IN STOKE-ON-TRENT, HULL & WOKING

Artistic Director: Ashley Page

NATIONAL TOUR
Light Fandango
Choreographer: Robert North
Composer: Ma / Meyer / O'Connor / Traditional Irish
Tzaikerk
Choreographer: Robert Cohan
Five Dances in the Manner of Isadora Duncan
Choreographer: Frederick Ashton
Composer: Brahms
The Two Pigeons (pas de deux)
Choreographer: Frederick Ashton
Composer: André Messager
Offenbach in the Underworld
Choreographer: Robert North
Composer: Offenbach / Stravinsky
Flower Festival at Genzano (pas de deux)
Choreographer: August Bournonville
Composer: Edvard Helsted
Troy Game
Choreographer: Robert North
Composer: Batucada / Downes
PERFORMED IN DUNFERMLINE, MUSSELBURGH, BARRA, BENBECULA, PORTREE, ULLAPOOL, STORNOWAY, DUMFRIES, GALASHIELS, MONTROSE, HADDO, STRANRAER, IRVINE, BERWICK-UPON-TWEED, OBAN & STIRLING

WINTER SEASON 2002/2003
The Snowman
Choreographer: Robert North
Composer: Howard Blake
PERFORMED IN GLASGOW, EDINBURGH, ABERDEEN, INVERNESS & HULL

2003–2005

2003
AUTUMN
Dangerous Liaisons
Choreographer: Richard Alston
Composer: Simon Waters
MiddleSexGorge
Choreographer: Stephen Petronio
Composer: Wire
White Man Sleeps
Choreographer: Siobhan Davies
Composer: Kevin Volans
Cheating Lying Stealing
Choreographer: Ashley Page
Composer: Lang / Gordon
Acrid Avid Jam
Choreographer: Ashley Page
Composer: Aphex Twin
Walking in the Heat
Choreographer: Ashley Page
Composer: Orlando Gough
PERFORMED IN EDINBURGH, GLASGOW, STIRLING & DUNDEE

THE NUTCRACKER 2003/2004
The Nutcracker
Choreographer: Ashley Page
Composer: Tchaikovsky
PERFORMED IN GLASGOW, ABERDEEN, INVERNESS, HULL & BELFAST

2004
SPRING SEASON
The Four Temperaments
Choreographer: George Balanchine
Composer: Paul Hindemith
Soft Underbelly
Choreographer: Ashley Page
Composer: Wim Mertens
Five Rückert Songs
Choreographer: Peter Darrell
Composer: Gustav Mahler / arr. Tovey
Acrid Avid Jam
Choreographer: Ashley Page
Composer: Aphex Twin
MiddleSexGorge
Choreographer: Stephen Petronio
Composer: Wire
32 Cryptograms
Choreographer: Ashley Page
Composer: Robert Moran
PERFORMED IN GLASGOW, EDINBURGH & INVERNESS

AUTUMN SEASON
Nightswimming into Day
Choreographer: Ashley Page
Composer: Eno / Schwalm / John Adams
Twilight
Choreographer: Hans van Manen
Composer: John Cage
Two Pieces for HET
Choreographer: Hans van Manen
Composer: Pärt / Tüür
Artifact Suite
Choreographer: William Forsythe
Composer: Bach / Crossman-Hecht
PERFORMED IN GLASGOW, EDINBURGH, INVERNESS & DUNDEE

THE NUTCRACKER 2004/2005
The Nutcracker
Choreographer: Ashley Page
Composer: Tchaikovsky
PERFORMED IN GLASGOW, EDINBURGH, INVERNESS & BELFAST

2005–2006

2005
SPRING SEASON
The Four Temperaments
Choreographer: George Balanchine
Composer: Paul Hindemith
Façade
Choreographer: Frederick Ashton
Composer: William Walton
Walking in the Heat
Choreographer: Ashley Page
Composer: Orlando Gough
The Pump Room
Choreographer: Ashley Page
Composer: Aphex Twin /
Nine Inch Nails
32 Cryptograms
Choreographer: Ashley Page
Composer: Robert Moran
PERFORMED IN GLASGOW,
EDINBURGH & INVERNESS

EDINBURGH
INTERNATIONAL FESTIVAL
Apollo
Choreographer: George Balanchine
Composer: Igor Stravinsky
Episodes
Choreographer: George Balanchine
Composer: Anton Webern
Rubies
Choreographer: George Balanchine
Composer: Igor Stravinsky

AUTUMN TOUR
Apollo
Choreographer: George Balanchine
Composer: Igor Stravinsky
Rubies
Choreographer: George Balanchine
Composer: Igor Stravinsky
The Pump Room
Choreographer: Ashley Page
Composer: Aphex Twin /
Nine Inch Nails
Walking in the Heat
Choreographer: Ashley Page
Composer: Orlando Gough
32 Cryptograms
Choreographer: Ashley Page
Composer: Robert Moran
PERFORMED IN ABERDEEN & STOKE

MERCHANT CITY FESTIVAL
Acrid Avid Jam
Choreographer: Ashley Page
Composer: Aphex Twin
Walking in the Heat
Choreographer: Ashley Page
Composer: Orlando Gough
The Pump Room
Choreographer: Ashley Page
Composer: Aphex Twin /
Nine Inch Nails
PERFORMED IN GLASGOW

CANADA PERFORMANCES
The Pump Room
Choreographer: Ashley Page
Composer: Nine Inch Nails /
Aphex Twin
PERFORMED IN TORONTO (CANADA)

CINDERELLA 2005/2006
Cinderella
Choreographer: Ashley Page
Composer: Sergei Prokofiev
PERFORMED IN GLASGOW,
EDINBURGH & ABERDEEN

2006

2006
CINDERELLA
Cinderella
Choreographer: Ashley Page
Composer: Sergei Prokofiev
PERFORMED IN STOKE-ON-TRENT
& LONDON

SPRING SEASON
Episodes
Choreographer: George Balanchine
Composer: Anton Webern
MiddleSexGorge
Choreographer: Stephen Petronio
Composer: Wire
Artifact Suite
Choreographer: William Forsythe
Composer: Bach / Crossman-Hecht
PERFORMED IN LONDON,
EDINBURGH & GLASGOW

EDINBURGH
INTERNATIONAL FESTIVAL
Agon
Choreographer: George Balanchine
Composer: Igor Stravinsky
Afternoon of A Faun
Choreographer: Jerome Robbins
Composer: Claude Debussy
Two Pieces for Het
Choreographer: Hans van Manen
Composer: Pärt / Tüür
In Light and Shadow
Choreographer: Krzysztof Pastor
Composer: Bach

AUTUMN TOUR
Refurbished Behaviour
Choreographer: Ashley Page
Composer: Wire / Andriessen
Acrid Avid Jam
Choreographer: Ashley Page
Composer: Aphex Twin /
Nine Inch Nails
Walking in the Heat
Choreographer: Ashley Page
Composer: Orlando Gough
Room of Cooks
Choreographer: Ashley Page
Composer: Orlando Gough
The Nutcracker Divertissements
Choreographer: Ashley Page
Composer: Tchaikovsky
Sirocco
Choreographer: Diana Loosmore
Composer: Ian Simmonds
Two Pieces for Het
Choreographer: Hans van Manen
Composer: Pärt / Tüür
The Pump Room
Choreographer: Ashley Page
Composer: Aphex Twin /
Nine Inch Nails
Agon
Choreographer: George Balanchine
Composer: Igor Stravinsky
Artifact Suite
Choreographer: William Forsythe
Composer: Bach / Crossman-Hecht
32 Cryptograms
Choreographer: Ashley Page
Composer: Robert Moran
PERFORMED IN PERTH, ULLAPOOL,
GALASHIELS, STRANRAER, STIRLING,
BERWICK-UPON-TWEED, ELGIN, OBAN,
STIRLING, GLASGOW & ABERDEEN

2006–2008

WINTER 2006/2007
CINDERELLA
Cinderella
Choreographer: Ashley Page
Composer: Sergei Prokofiev
PERFORMED IN GLASGOW, EDINBURGH,
BELFAST, ABERDEEN & CARDIFF

2007
SPRING
Agon
Choreographer: George Balanchine
Composer: Igor Stravinsky
Room of Cooks
Choreographer: Ashley Page
Composer: Orlando Gough
Othello
Choreographer: Peter Darrell
Composer: Franz Liszt
In Light and Shadow
Choreographer: Krzysztof Pastor
Composer: Bach
Chasing Ghosts
Choreographer: Diana Loosmore
Composer: Ian Simmonds
PERFORMED IN GLASGOW,
EDINBURGH & ABERDEEN

EDINBURGH
INTERNATIONAL FESTIVAL
Ride the Beast
Choreographer: Stephen Petronio
Composer: Radiohead
For MG: The Movie
Choreographer: Trisha Brown
Composer: Alvin Curran
Fearful Symmetries
Choreographer: Ashley Page
Composer: John Adams

AUTUMN
Fearful Symmetries
Choreographer: Ashley Page
Composer: John Adams
Apollo
Choreographer: George Balanchine
Composer: Igor Starvinsky
Chasing Ghosts
Choreographer: Diana Loosmore
Composer: Ian Simmonds
Afternoon of a Faun
Choreographer: Jerome Robbins
Composer: Claude Debussy
PERFORMED IN ABERDEEN

WINTER 2007/2008
THE SLEEPING BEAUTY
The Sleeping Beauty
Choreographer: Ashley Page /
Marius Petipa
Composer: Tchaikovsky
PERFORMED IN GLASGOW, EDINBURGH,
ABERDEEN, INVERNESS & NEWCASTLE

2008
ROMEO & JULIET
Romeo & Juliet
Choreographer: Krzysztof Pastor
Composer: Sergei Prokofiev
PERFORMED IN EDINBURGH, ABERDEEN,
INVERNESS & GLASGOW

SUMMER
Othello
Choreographer: Peter Darrell
Composer: Franz Liszt
Träume
Choreographer: Gregory Dean
Composer: Colleen

2008–2009

Ride the Beast
Choreographer: Stephen Petronio
Composer: Radiohead
In Light and Shadow
Choreographer: Krzysztof Pastor
Composer: J.S. Bach
Lull
Choreographer: Diana Loosmore
Composer: Basquiat Strings
PERFORMED IN ULLAPOOL,
BERWICK-UPON-TWEED, STORNOWAY,
STRANRAER, KIRKWALL, GALASHIELS,
LERWICK, ST ANDREWS, ELGIN, FORFAR,
ABERDEEN, OBAN & DUMFRIES

AUTUMN
Ride the Beast
Choreographer: Stephen Petronio
Composer: Radiohead
For MG: The Movie
Choreographer: Trisha Brown
Composer: Alvin Curran
Pennies From Heaven
Choreographer: Ashley Page
Composer: 1930s Popular Music
PERFORMED IN GLASGOW, EDINBURGH,
LONDON, INVERNESS & ABERDEEN

WINTER 2008/2009
THE SLEEPING BEAUTY
The Sleeping Beauty
Choreographer: Ashley Page /
Marius Petipa
Composer: Tchaikovsky
PERFORMED IN GLASGOW,
EDINBURGH, INVERNESS,
CARDIFF, ABERDEEN & BELFAST

2009
SPRING
Carmen
Choreographer: Richard Alston
Composer: Rodion Shchedrin
after Bizet
Cheating Lying Stealing
Choreographer: Ashley Page
Composer: Gordon / Lang
PERFORMED IN GLASGOW, EDINBURGH,
ABERDEEN & INVERNESS

CHINA TOUR
Carmen
Choreographer: Richard Alston
Composer: Rodion Shchedrin
after Bizet
Pennies from Heaven
Choreographer: Ashley Page
Composer: 1930s Popular Music
PERFORMED IN NANJING, SHANGHAI
& BEIJING (CHINA)

EDINBURGH
INTERNATIONAL FESTIVAL
Scènes de Ballet
Choreographer: Frederick Ashton
Composer: Igor Stravinsky
Workwithinwork
Choreographer: William Forsythe
Composer: Luciano Berio
Petrushka
Choreographer: Ian Spink
Composer: Igor Stravinsky
PERFORMED IN EDINBURGH

40TH ANNIVERSARY SEASON
Rubies
Choreographer: George Balanchine
Composer: Igor Stravinsky

2009

Workwithinwork
Choreographer: William Forsythe
Composer: Luciano Berio
In Light and Shadow
Choreographer: Krzysztof Pastor
Composer: Bach
PERFORMED IN LONDON, GLASGOW,
EDINBURGH, ABERDEEN & INVERNESS

INDEX

ACKNOWLEDGMENTS AND PHOTOGRAPHY CREDITS

EDITOR: Sara Hunt
ASSOCIATE EDITORS: Ann Nugent and Charlotte Gross
DESIGN: Deborah White
EDITORIAL ASSISTANTS: Heather Crumley and Sara Myers

The author and publisher would like to thank the following people for their generous assistance, advice, comments and time spent helping in various ways during the preparation of this book: Cindy Sughrue, Ashley Page, Paul Tyers and all at Scottish Ballet; Rosemary James for research; Claire McKendrick, Sharon Lawler and Neill Miller of the University of Glasgow Library, Special Collections Department; and Elaine Lucas of the V&A.

We have told the story of Scottish Ballet's first four decades primarily through memorable photographs, and our profound thanks are due to the photographers whose extraordinary work is showcased in these pages. The photographers are listed below, with the page numbers on which their images appear. All photographs taken before 2002 are reproduced by courtesy of either the Scottish Ballet Archive or the University of Glasgow Library Special Collections Department (Scottish Ballet Collection). In a small number of cases, no information has been discovered as to the photographer of the particular image selected (in which case, the images are simply credited to these sources); or we have been unable to locate the credited photographers (or their heirs) to request permission for reproduction, despite making every effort to do so. For any errors or omissions we have made, we sincerely apologise, and we welcome the opportunity to correct the records: please submit any queries to the publisher.

© **Catherine Ashmore**: 104–5
Bryan & Shear Ltd: 45br
© **Bill Cooper**: 7, 13, 24b, 26-27, 28, 29l, 29tr, 30(both), 41 (both), 44tl, 44r, 47, 48, 49b, 57, 58, 61, 78, 79, 81, 82, 83, 106, 108, 109, 110–11, 114, 115, 116–17, 118, 119, 120, 121, 141, 146
© **Anthony Crickmay**/V&A Images/V&A Theatre Collections: 10, 11 (both), 12b, 16, 17, 18b, 19, 20l, 21, 65, 66, 68–69, 72, 85
© **Alan Crumlish**: 22, 25b, 32bl, 36t, 39l, 39br
© **Will Davidson**: 164
© **Drew Farrell**: 20r, 40bl, 42tl & r, 43, 75
© **Wil Freeborn**: 50b
© **Sasha Gusov**: 76, 77
© **Chris Harris**: 39tr
© **Merlin Hendy**: 2, 53, 173, 174, 180, 181
By courtesy of **The Herald**: 25t; The Herald, photo by Arthur Kinlock: 31
© **David Liddle**: 33
© **Alistair Livingstone**: 12t

© **William Long**: 15, 32tl, 34tl and cl, 37, 38, 70
© **Kevin Low**: 45t, 80
© **Antonia Reeve**: 23, 36b
© **Andrew Ross**: 46 both, 49t, 50tl & tr, 51 both, 52 both, 55, 87, 88, 89, 90-91, 92, 93, 94, 95, 96, 97, 98, 99, 100, 101, 102-103, 107, 112, 113, 122–23, 124–25, 126–27, 129, 130–31, 132, 133, 136, 138, 139, 140, 142, 143, 144, 145, 147, 148, 149, 151, 152, 153, 154, 155, 156–57, 158–59, 160, 162–63, 166, 167, 168–69, 170, 175, 176–77, 178–79
© **Roy Round**: 73
By courtesy of **Scottish Ballet**: 8, 18tl, 24tl & tc, 29b, 42b, 44bl, 63, 84
© **Diane Tammes**: 14
© **Eric Thorburn**: 40tl, 40r
By courtesy of **University of Glasgow, Special Collections Department**: 34bl & br
© **George Wilkie/Wilfoto**: 9, 34tr, 35
© **C.H. Wood**: 64
© **Graham Wylie**: 135